T0318964

Bulletproof Decisions

Bulletproof Decisions

How Executives Can
Get It Right, Every Time

Ruben Ugarte

Routledge
Taylor & Francis Group

A PRODUCTIVITY PRESS BOOK

First published 2022
by Routledge
605 Third Avenue, New York, NY 10158

and by Routledge
2 Park Square, Milton Park, Abingdon, Oxon, OX14 4RN

Routledge is an imprint of the Taylor & Francis Group, an informa business

ISBN: 9781032028262 (hbk)
ISBN: 9781032028255 (pbk)
ISBN: 9781003185383 (ebk)

DOI: 10.4324/9781003185383

Typeset in Bembo
by Deanta Global Publishing Services, Chennai, India

Dedication

To all those who have written, spoken, thought, and debated on the value of better decisions. I thank you for the shoulders to stand on.

Contents

Author

Ruben Ugarte is an expert in data and decision-making and is the author of *Data Mirage: Why Companies Fail to Actually Use Their Data*. He has helped over 75 medium-sized and large enterprises, including the Fortune 1000, across five continents, use data to make higher quality decisions.

These decisions help companies significantly boost performance, increase profitability, dramatically lower costs, and make their teams world-class. He also maintains a popular blog that has more than 100,000 readers. In his free time, you can find him dancing or trying to learn something new. He lives in Vancouver, Canada.

Introduction

The power of decisions has been debated for centuries. The Greeks and Romans used to think that their circle of influence was limited. The Greeks refused to sail toward Troy until the Gods told them that it was safe. To entice the gods, rituals and sacrifices had to be done. Agamemnon—King of Mycenae and brother of Menelaus (whose wife was Helen)—famously sacrificed his own daughter to ensure safe passage to Troy. Agamemnon couldn't simply decide to sail, he needed permission from the gods.

The Romans maintained the same practice, and early forms of Christianity built upon it. Humans could decide minor things like what to eat or wear, but you were operating within a constrained world ruled by the Gods (or the one God for Christians). It would be crazy to think that your decisions were completely within your control. Blasphemous perhaps. Armies that did well in the war gave credit to the gods and less so to their strategic decisions.

Fast forward to our modern world, and we have swung to the other extreme. We now believe that we are and should be fully in control of our decisions. Our life unfolds based on the decisions that we make. Each one creates a branch that could take our lives in unexpected directions. If your life isn't going well, then you need to reconsider the decisions that you're making. Children are told to choose wisely, as the world is their oyster. No need to look toward the Gods, as their influence on our world is non-existent.

I'm a product of this world, and I lean more toward this new world. I don't think everything is within our control, but I think we make the most out of every situation. There are always options to the challenges that we face, though we may not like our options. Increasing the control (at least in perception) is a worthy goal. We may not be able to control when it rains, but we can carry an umbrella. We may not control what other people do but can operate within our circle of influence.

Naturally, our increased perception of control over our decisions means that we should spend time understanding how the skill of decision-making can be improved. Like many things, decision-making is a process that can be applied to many types of content. The decisions you make at work and the decisions you make in your personal life are similar. You can follow steps to optimize both of these categories (and you should!). This book is my attempt to provide you with optimization strategies.

I wrote this book for executives based on my work. I help companies use data to make better decisions, and I have seen firsthand how decisions get made (or don't get made) in companies. You can't simply look at the facts and decide. There's a complex background of biases, preferences, and conflicts that are interwoven with every decision. Companies and people can swing between making amazing and terrible decisions. For some of my clients, decision-making felt like a black box. Sometimes it worked, sometimes it didn't.

As I wrote this book, I realized that the principles could apply to decisions outside of work. In fact, my clients needed to think holistically about their decisions. There's no point in doing well at work while your personal life crumbles. Failing to make the right decisions at work can lead to lost revenue, lost customers, and perhaps even a lost job. In your personal life, it could lead to strained relationships, health concerns, and general unhappiness.

Our modern life has forced us to deal with hundreds and thousands of decisions every day. Some are small, like choosing what to wear, and some are large, like choosing what markets to enter as a business. The challenge is that each decision consumes mental energy, and it can add up. By the time lunch hits, you might be mentally exhausted even if you made "small" decisions. Tiny decisions shouldn't be dismissed either. Choosing what to eat for lunch is minor, but it can add up to significant issues for your health if you consistently make the wrong decision every day.

I came up with three strategies for dealing with the barrage of decisions that comes your way every day: elimination, automation, optimization. The first strategy will help us eliminate a huge chunk of decisions through effective problem-solving. The second strategy will help us automate decisions that are important but repetitive. The third strategy will be used to tackle the "critical few" decisions that require all your mental energy. I'll do my best to share professional and personal examples to explain each strategy. As you think through these strategies, keep in mind the following 2 × 2 chapter on decision importance and complexity (Figure I.1).

Decision Importance vs Complexity

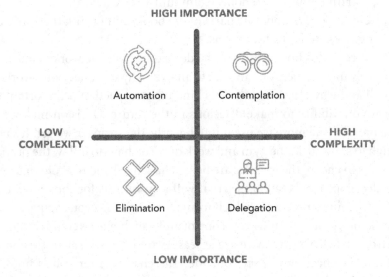

FIGURE I.1
Decision importance and complexity.

The importance and complexity of a decision shape how we should approach it. Decisions with high importance and complexity require contemplation. High complexity but low importance can be delegated—an option within the elimination strategy. Low importance and low complexity should be eliminated altogether. Low complexity but high importance should be automated—strategy #2 in our book. The third strategy, optimization, will help you the most with the decisions that fall into the top right quadrant.

The other chapters will provide ideas to help better understand the nuances of decisions. What are the different forces which change how we approach decisions? When should you involve your team in decisions? What role does morality play in decisions? These questions and more are answered through the book. What may seem like a simple topic is endlessly fascinating. We don't typically get a formal education in decisions, and this is the book that bridges that gap.

Every chapter also has sections called "Behind the Decision." Each section looks at a pivotal decision that has shaped our world today. We can go back in time and see how the decisions of certain people ended up having a significant impact on their world (and ours). I look at Renaissance Popes, Martin Luther, the iPhone, Communism in Cuba, and much more. They were some of my favorite parts of the book, and I think they provide a larger context to look at decisions.

As you read this book, think of the decisions that have worked out well and poorly in your life. You can start to analyze why some decisions worked out well and why others didn't. This kind of retrospection is important to improve our ability to make decisions in the future. Decision-making is like a muscle. The more we use it intelligently, the stronger we get. It's not enough to show up at the gym and work out. You have to follow the proper workouts to ensure the muscles are being challenged and to avoid injuries. Poor decisions can create biases that will stay with us for the rest of our lives. By having a process in which to analyze decisions, you can parse out what elements were within your control and which ones weren't

I strongly believe that there are at least two to three ideas in this book that can significantly impact your life. The challenge for you is finding and applying them. You might only read certain chapters, and you might find that some portions aren't well suited for you. Focus on looking for the things relevant to you, and don't assume that you have to internalize the entire book. I'm excited to see how your decision-making process evolves and the role these ideas might play.

Let's get started.

Ruben Ugarte
Vancouver, Canada

Other Works by Ruben Ugarte

THE DATA MIRAGE: WHY COMPANIES FAIL TO ACTUALLY USE THEIR DATA

The Data Mirage is a business book for executives and leaders who want to unlock more insights from their data and make better decisions. The importance of data doesn't need an introduction or a fancy pitch deck. Data plays a critical role in helping companies to better understand their users, beat out their competitors, and break through their growth targets.

However, despite significant investments in their data, most organizations struggle to get much value from it. According to Forrester, only 38% of senior executives and decision-makers "have a high level of confidence in their customer insights and only 33% trust the analytics they generate from their business operations."

This reflects the real world that I have experienced. In this book, I help readers formulate an analytics strategy that works in the real world, show them how to think about KPIs, and help them tackle the problems they are bound to come across as they try to use data to make better decisions.

1

35,000 Reasons Why You Need This Book

From the moment you open your eyes in the morning, you start making decisions. Should you hit the snooze button one more time or get started with your day? What clothes should you wear? Do you have enough time for breakfast, or should you get something on the way to work? On some days, these kinds of decisions are a breeze. On other days, it feels like every decision is a slog through enemy territory.

There's a popular statistic out there that states that we make 35,000 decisions every single day*. I can't seem to find the math behind this eye-popping number, but the reality is that we make many decisions on an average day. Some are inconsequential, but others can affect hundreds and thousands of other people. A decision to go into a new market could fail and result in loss of jobs.

Think back on your day today and go through the major decisions that took place in your life. As an executive, your entire job is to make decisions, especially at a strategic level. How comfortable do you feel in your process of making decisions? Does that process always work as expected? Do you even know what process is playing out in your mind?

It's also important to consider the seemingly small decisions. The morning coffee, what to eat for lunch, and what time you are going to the gym. These decisions may not seem as important as deciding who to hire for your team, but they can take up as much, if not more, mental energy. Worse of all, failing to make these seemingly small decisions can lead to

---

* "Basis for 'We Make 35,000 Decisions a Day' Statistic," StackExchange, accessed January 10, 2021, https://psychology.stackexchange.com/questions/17182/basis-for-we-make-35-000-decisions-a-day-statistic.

DOI: 10.4324/9781003185383-1

long-term stress. Think about how frustrating it can be to struggle to lose weight and the series of decisions that lead to this outcome.

This book is meant to help you take control of the most important decisions in your life. I say life because I think our professional and personal worlds are heavily intertwined these days. There's no point in making improvements to our decisions at work if our marriage is failing. The spillover from our personal life will eventually affect our work and vice versa.

I can't promise that you'll get better at all the 35,000 decisions (or whatever the actual number is), but even improving by 1% can be significant over a period of time. This is the philosophy behind one of my mentors, Alan Weiss*. If you improve by 1% every day, in 70 days, you'll be twice as good.

Making better decisions is great, but knowing how you make the best decisions is a game-changer. You're bound to come across situations that you have never seen before. It could be a tricky family dilemma or an ethical challenge. You can't prepare for every possible decision you will make in your life, but you can adopt frameworks that can be applied in any situation. The major framework is called the 3 Os, which we will explore in the upcoming chapters.

I love asking executives about major decisions that went well and wrong. As a side note, this is another theme for this book. I'm not just interested in the wrong decisions but the right ones. I want to know why something went right and how to replicate that instead of trying to fix "errors in judgment."

Some executives tell me that they don't have a formal decision-making process. They simply "go with their gut" or recollect that they "thought about it and then made a decision." In reality, there's always a process behind the scenes whenever we make a decision. We just don't know what it is, or we are unable to articulate it.

This opaqueness is my workday today, but it also limits you whenever you come across a decision that doesn't fit nicely into your existing mental models. If you think about work and your life, you could likely think about categories of decisions that seem harder to you. These categories may be affected by hidden biases that derail you without you knowing it.

---

* "Compound Interest," Blog, Alan Weiss, accessed January 10, 2021, https://alanweiss.com/compound-interest/.

In this book, my goal is to help you surface your hidden decision-making process and make some upgrades to it. You can adopt my 3 Os framework or take elements from it and make it your own. Either way, you should strive to feel more comfortable making tough decisions and increasing the speed you make them.

IT'S THE NOT THE QUANTITY BUT THE MENTAL BURDEN

When I was preparing to write this book, I became fascinated by that 35,000 number from the previous section. Everyone with whom I shared that number was also equally taken back. As I mentioned, it's a big number that might not actually be based on any hard evidence. However, this got me thinking about the costs of decisions.

We don't typically have to pay someone to make a decision. We can decide to have pasta or a burger for lunch, but we don't have to pay anyone if we make the wrong decision. Wrong, in this case, would be an afternoon slump or feeling guilty because we broke our diet. This decision in isolation doesn't seem like a big deal. It takes a few seconds, and then you move on with your life.

However, I realize that decisions on their own are rarely life-changing. There are exceptions to this, of course, such as deciding to marry your partner or accepting a job offer where you will have to move across the country. These are the exceptions that prove the rule. We don't make these kinds of decisions every single day. An executive will make more of these "significant" decisions in their day-to-day life, but they will also make smaller decisions.

The problem is that all decisions, large or small, can create a mental burden on our lives. They can tire us mentally of having to make decisions constantly. Think about how you feel after a long day at work filled with back-to-back meetings, complaints, and conversations. You get home, and you have to decide what to eat. This "simple" decision could feel incredibly hard, and you may end up browsing through the food delivery app for 15 minutes just trying to figure out what to eat. It's not that ordering food is hard but that your mental capacity for making decisions has been depleted throughout the day.

This is where the adage of "don't make important decisions late in the day" comes from. For most of us, we get more mentally tired as the day progresses. Decisions that would seem trivial in the morning can seem insurmountable in the afternoon. There was a study done in 2011 that found that court judges made more positive rulings at the beginning of their day or right after a meal break like lunch.* If you're going to face a judge for a criminal ruling, you should strive to schedule your meeting as early in the day as possible!

We can also see the impact of bad decisions play out in the corporate world every day. At the start of 2021, Intel had to replace its CEO after years of poor performance and losing the top position in the chip manufacturing business.† We shouldn't even talk about the previous CEO being fired for having an affair with a subordinate. When executives make the wrong decisions, it doesn't just affect them. These decisions are compounded further by each employee and reported under them.

The new Intel CEO has decided to retake the lead in the chip manufacturing space. This won't be easy, especially as Apple is moving away from Intel with its M1 chip. TSMC continues to dominate the space, and other competitors are taking further market share from Intel. Regardless of what the Intel CEO decides, they will have to make the right decisions in an uncertain climate.

Another example of how bad decisions can compound in unexpected ways is Volkswagen. After five years of anticipation, they released the ID.3, their first answer to Tesla. Despite a 50 Billion dollar investment, the car was full of bugs.‡ Most of the fancy features touted in the roll-up weren't there, and the engineers haven't been able to figure out how to update the software remotely. This comes on the heels of the poorly launched Golf-8 and the cheating scandal for tracking diesel emissions.

It's not all bad news for Volkswagen, as their ID.3 is starting to outsell Tesla in Europe. They are in the middle of a seismic shift trying to convert a hardware-driven car marker into a software-driven one. They are also

---

* "Extraneous Factors in Judicial Decisions," PNAS, accessed January 16, 2021, https://www.pnas.org/content/108/17/6889.
† "Intel's New Chief Has No Quick Fix," *Wall Street Journal*, accessed January 14, 2021, https://www.wsj.com/articles/intels-new-chief-has-no-quick-fix-11610562666.
‡ "How Volkswagen's $50 Billion Plan to Beat Tesla Short-Circuited," *Wall Street Journal*, accessed January 14, 2021,https://www.wsj.com/articles/how-volkswagens-50-billion-plan-to-beat-tesla-short-circuited-11611073974

outspending any other automakers and doing their best to catch up to Tesla.

Everything seems clearer in hindsight, and we can always look at other companies' mistakes and say, "that was a dumb decision." The reality is that sometimes things only make sense once you're outside the forest. When you're inside, you can also see trees for as far as the eye can see.

This book is meant to help you find a way through all the trees without using hindsight. Once you get better at it, you can then work with your team to help them make better decisions. We all know that strategy always looks perfect when formulated in workshops, but it can transform into something completely different once it reaches the person putting screws on the cars.

Bad decisions aren't just harmful to the person that made them. They create what I call the "Loop of Regret," which shows how "bad" decisions are compounded and the effects of being in this loop (Figure 1.1).

I put "bad" in quotes because we often don't know that a bad decision was made until after the fact. Nonetheless, "bad" decisions become worse decisions later on. The poor choices made at Intel limit what people down the chain can do. Their decisions will be worse merely by the limiting factor of the loop. Once you're in the loop, you have fewer options, emotions run higher, and you need high energy to escape the loop. A higher energy action is a CEO being replaced or divorcing your spouse.

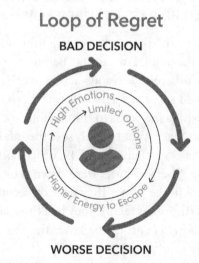

FIGURE 1.1
Loop of regret.

In some cases, you are forced upon a Loop of Regret. Think of any executive that took the reins of a company in trouble or anyone who's ever had to deal with a negative family situation. You can recognize once you're in this loop and then determine what high energy or "tough" decisions need to be made. These decisions are some of the toughest because there's usually limited upside, high risk, and the need to navigate through the emotions of everyone involved.

Going back to the mental burden of decisions, this is also why I can't separate personal work from work. Everything is interconnected, and we need to view it as a whole. If you improved your decisions only at work, you would still run into a mental burden whenever you had to think about your family, your health, what to eat, and other personal questions. It's common for me to meet executives who are doing quite well at work, but their personal lives are in disarray.

I'm interested in figuring out how to make the post-work food decision and every other decision easy. What do you need to do during the day that will make your decisions consistent and effective at any time? This is where we start talking about strategies for how to handle decisions. We'll group them into three major categories, and each category will have a different strategy or approach.

BEHIND THE DECISION: SEAHAWKS FAILED PASS IN SUPER BOWL 49

Before talking about the three strategies, let me introduce you to a special section in this book I'm calling "Behind the Decision." I will take you through different decisions across sports, work, and anything else that could serve as a lesson for us. Each of these sections will provide you with a few ideas to think about and internalize.

The first decision that I want to analyze is the infamous failed pass by the Seattle Seahawks in Super Bowl 49, which cost them the game and championship. The Seahawks were down four points with less than 30 seconds left in the game. They were on second down and the Patriots' one-yard (the other team). They had three attempts (second, third, and fourth down) to get the ball over the end goal and win the game.

You should also know that the Seahawks had the best running back that season, Marshawn Lynch. For most people, this means that giving the ball to him and running it through the end goal was the most logical play. Instead, the Seahawks quarterback Russell Wilson threw the ball as a pass, and it got intercepted. Game over for the Seahawks.

Let's look at the options that could have taken place here:

1. Pass the ball on second down
2. Run it with Marshawn Lynch
3. Kick it for a field goal worth three points

Option three is out immediately since it wouldn't be enough to tie or win the game, and there wasn't enough time to get the ball back. Option two is what most people consider logical, and option one is what actually happened.

Let's look at some stats to see how likely option one or option two was to succeed. In that season, 66 passes (option one) from the one-yard line were thrown and intercepted one time which happened on this exact pass. This means that 65 passes had been thrown from the one-yard with no interceptions before this play happened.[*]

There's also a strategic point here. The Seahawks couldn't run the ball three times in a row. The Patriots' defense would adjust so they could run the ball once or twice at most. This meant passing the ball on the second down seemed like a good option. Passing the ball had three potential outcomes: scoring, incomplete pass, or interception. Two of the three options were good, while one option was catastrophic.

As we can see, passing the ball on a second down wasn't a crazy choice. It made rational sense and had a high probability of success. It just happened that the low odds of failure also meant complete failure. If the Seahawks got a chance to redo this play, it would still make sense to pass the ball. If that pass fails, they could run it in the third and fourth down.

The lesson here is that you can't let fear derail your decision-making. You need to make the best possible decision based on what you know (data and assumptions) and try to minimize the risks as much as possible. Make decisions based on an expectation of success and not failure.

---

[*] "Twitter," Twitter, accessed January 19, 2021, https://twitter.com/SandoNFL/status/562134369 025163265

As a general note, this example is also the first time that we get to see the 3 Os framework in action. This framework stands for Outcomes, Options, and Obstacles. Read through the example again and look for these three elements in the Seahawks decision and how they handle each one.

3 STRATEGIES FOR DEALING WITH DECISIONS

There are three strategies for dealing with many decisions in our lives: problem-solving, the turtleneck principle, and the 3 Os. Each one has a different role, and while you can take any of them and improve your decision-making, adopting all of them is where the real power lies.

The first strategy, problem-solving, is exclusively focused on understanding the problem or questions you're trying to solve. The field of problem-solving has been around since the dawn of humanity. We are problem-solving machines, and you could even see evolution as a form of problem-solving, as species try to figure out how to adapt to their changing conditions.

I use the word problem solving because it is a widely recognized term, but don't get caught in its negative connotations. You could also use the same ideas to figure out how to innovate in your business or do new things. The reality is the best companies aren't just interested in solving problems. My best clients don't have "problems"; instead, they are doing well, and they want to learn how to do even better. Things aren't perfect, but they also aren't broken.

I think the same idea applies to people. We now hear of "first world problems" to describe the annoyances that some of us experience living in highly developed countries. Complaining about a late Amazon delivery may seem trivial when thinking about people who don't have access to running water or live in the middle of civil wars. Nonetheless, we'll use the term problem-solving, but it's merely a way of figuring out what we should be doing and where we should focus on our resources.

The second strategy, the turtleneck principle, is my own term for a category of decisions that only need to be made once. I named it after Steve Jobs, who famously only wore black turtlenecks to work. He decided what "uniform" he should wear and then simply executed that decision every day. There are countless decisions like this every day that we don't want to make but feel forced to do.

On the personal side, these decisions could include what to wear, what to eat, when to workout, and what to watch at night. On the work side, they could include when your team meets next, where to get the latest information, and what to work on next. The common thread behind all of these decisions is that we can simply make them once and then schedule them into our lives. This reduces the burn and increases the likelihood of them actually taking place. This chapter could explain why you tend to procrastinate on going to the gym or tackle certain kinds of work.

The third strategy, the 3 Os, is the framework for the chosen few, the most important decisions can't be automated or tackled merely through problem-solving. You need to think about them, consider the options, and proactively tackle obstacles. I created a three step framework that you can adapt to your own needs. I'm skeptical of any framework that is highly complicated. I kept seeing decision-making frameworks that had nine steps and four sub-steps and would take three months. We need to make decisions quickly and effectively, and I think simplicity is the key here.

Beyond these three strategies, we'll also explore other ideas for integrating these ideas into your teams and your life. I also included a chapter on ethics, which tends to color some of the toughest decisions you will ever make, especially as an executive. Throughout the entire book, I'll do my best to include contemporary examples and decision breakdowns to show the ideas in action. My goal is for this book to be practical and relevant, not just a theoretical approach to making better decisions.

BEHIND THE DECISION: SWEDEN'S UNORTHODOX COVID-19 STRATEGY

As we learned more about the COVID-19 pandemic, every country started imposing lockdown restrictions that ranged from mild to one step away from martial law. One country that stood apart from everyone was Sweden. From the very beginning, they said they wouldn't impose sweeping restrictions and instead would rely on herd immunity to deal with the virus. The strategy was put forth by the Swedish Public Health Organization, and they defended it from internal and external criticism.

A key figure in the development of this strategy was Anders Tegnell, who said the following when asked about this approach,

> "Sweden has gone mostly for voluntary measures because that's how we're used to working, and we have a long tradition that it works rather well. So far, it's been working reasonably well."*

By the end of March 2020, Sweden's strategy looked quite good. Sweden had 3,700 confirmed cases of COVID-19 and recorded 110 deaths. In contrast, Italy had over 100,000 cases and 10,000 deaths, and Spain had 80,000 cases and 6,500 deaths. Even when taking into account the population size, the difference was staggering. While its neighbors lived under strict restrictions and curfew, the Swedes were going about their lives as if nothing was happening.

As you can imagine, things didn't continue to go as well for Sweden. By December 20, 2020, COVID-19 deaths in Sweden had reached more than 8,000 or five to ten times their Nordic neighbors. In early January 2021, Sweden moved to impose a mandatory face mask restriction, limited school instruction, and close down non-essential shops. The king of Sweden, Carl XVI Gustaf, said that "we have failed" just before Christmas 2020. The one silver lining is that the Swedish economy wasn't as severely affected as its neighbors but still saw "record level" contractions and drops.

The reasons for why the Sweden approach failed are only now starting to surface. We now know that wearing masks is quite effective in reducing the spread of COVID-19. We also know that there are high-risk activities that should be limited or canceled. We also know that people will adjust to their restrictions as long as they are clear. In Sweden, it was recommended to limit social contact, but people were being left to guess what this actually meant without specific restrictions.

For our analysis, we can see that Sweden made a drastically different decision than almost everyone else. They looked at the limited data in March 2020 and concluded that a severe lockdown wasn't needed. They didn't expect how the virus would spread within their communities or that other conditions would change around them. It's hard to fault them for their actions, but there are lessons to be learned here.

---

* "No Lockdown Here: Sweden Defends Its More Relaxed Coronavirus Strategy," CNBC, accessed January 25, 2021, https://www.cnbc.com/2020/03/30/sweden-coronavirus-approach-is-very-different-from-the-rest-of-europe.html

If you're not sure of the exact outcome of your decision, but you know that some of the possibilities could have severe negative consequences, you need to take stronger preventive action. This concept of preventing and contingent actions is one of my favorites, and I will explain it later on in the book. I learned it from one of my mentors, Alan Weiss, and I think it's a fantastic way of dealing with uncertainty.

YES, INACTION IS A DECISION

I also want to highlight an important element of any decision. It's sometimes easier to put off deciding while we "collect more information" or "sleep on it." Prudence is fine but remember that inaction is a decision. Even if we don't actively decide, we have already made the decision. Inaction can be one of the worst decisions because we don't control the outcomes. Simply letting things play out can be a stress-inducing recipe.

Do note that inaction is different from dealing with reasonable risk. Every day, we make decisions that put us in harm's way. We drive to work, we get on airplanes, and we interact with other humans. In any of these situations, we could face high levels of risk and even death. Car crashes, flying accidents, and even pandemics are around us all the time. If we only took action whenever there was no risk, we would never leave our house or even our room!

There are also situations where you gauge the risk of a decision, and you will conclude that the risk is worthwhile or low enough to deal with it. Think about fire safety. If a building or our home caught fire, it could be devastating. We don't live in paralysis at the thought that at any moment, we may find ourselves in the middle of a fire. Instead, we take reasonable actions by putting water sprinklers and fire alarms into our homes and buildings. If a fire takes place, we hope that these measures would be sufficient.

Inaction tends to be associated with highly emotional or uncertain decisions. Think about climate change and how uncertain and complex this challenge is. For most countries, it requires a seismic shift in the design of their economies. A country like Germany needs to figure out what to do with industries like coal, which makes up 35% of their energy sources as of late 2020. How do you shift all the workers and companies that operate in this space while also dealing with climate change?

The answers aren't easy, and it's much easier to do nothing than figure it out. Germany, to its credit, is doing their best to hit its emission targets. They have found ways of shutting down mines, finding work for laid-off workers, or offering them retirement packages. Germany has been in the process of phasing out coal for more than 40 years.

In your life, take stock of areas where inaction has been the primary decision. It's not helpful to beat ourselves up as to why we didn't do something. Instead, we need to look for patterns and try to uncover new ways of doing something. Ask yourself the following questions to better understand why these areas have led to inaction:

- Are there any obvious patterns in these areas? They could all be in your personal life or related to the same people or similar situations.
- Why was inaction easier than making a decision?
- Are there high emotions associated with this decision?
- Do I have a high level of confidence in the potential outcomes of this decision?

Inaction also gets tougher with time. The longer that we have been putting off a decision, the harder it can feel. This is similar to the Loop of Regret, where we will experience fewer options and higher emotions as time goes on. The first step is recognizing where inaction is taking place and then deciding what needs to happen to get out of this loop.

NOT EVERY DECISION HAS A HAPPY OUTCOME

It's also important to recognize that not every decision has a "positive" outcome. In fact, the hardest decisions that you will face will be choices between two "negative" outcomes. The goal isn't to always maximize happiness or to minimize pain. The goal is to make the right decisions based on all the factors involved. Some decisions will be right but will feel incredibly painful or hard.

Let's go back to COVID-19. It's easy to be an armchair quarterback and comment on the decisions made by governments. The reality is that every single government is forced to choose from two outcomes: saving lives or saving the economy. Lockdowns and restrictions save lives, but they destroy the economy and the livelihoods of some people. The economic effect isn't felt consistently across everyone, but industries like restaurants and hotels suffered significantly.

I got a chance to work with the tourism side of the British Columbia provincial government and helped them sort through all their data to understand better how they should make decisions. They also wanted to share this data with their partners, including hotels, restaurants, and other major tourism businesses around the province. We designed a dashboard that would summarize the most important KPIs into a single page and help anyone understand how the pandemic affected the industry.

The numbers were released publicly, and they were bleak. Hotel occupancy in major cities hovered around 30%, travelers coming into the country were down to nearly nothing, and even residents weren't traveling within the province. This wasn't a surprise since that's exactly what the provincial restrictions were meant to do. For businesses in this industry, all the choices were hard. Without knowing when things would change, businesses were simply trying to survive by minimizing expenses and relying on government financial support, which the Canadian government rapidly deployed.

The best decision frameworks in the world wouldn't make the situation better. However, making better decisions can position them for success in the near future. What are the opportunities that are hiding in front of them? How will traveler behaviors change, and how can they adjust to them? Are there areas for innovation in how travel is expected?

These questions aren't usually a high priority when you're simply trying to run your business and make the most out of the current demand. The vacuum in travelers allows businesses to think about the future and how to best prepare for it. The impact of those decisions will be felt. The quality of decisions made today will become exponentially relevant in the next three to five years. I expect that we will hear stories of businesses that adjusted well to the pandemic and others that didn't.

In your personal life, hard decisions can also be the most important. Choosing to hit the gym or skip on dessert can feel hard, but it may be incredibly helpful in ten years when you're avoiding major health issues. Choosing to pass on a work opportunity to spend more time with your family can save your mental health and relationships. These are the decisions that we need the most help with because they are the ones that truly matter.

CHAPTER SUMMARY

- It doesn't matter how many decisions you make every day. Getting better at making the right decisions is one of the best ways to level up your work and personal life.
- The mental burden of making decisions is the same whether you're trying to choose what to eat or what market to enter next.
- Don't let rare possibilities derail your decision-making. Make decisions expecting success and adjust accordingly.
- Inaction is a decision. The issue is that you can't always control the consequences of inaction.
- Not every decision will have a happy or positive outcome, but that doesn't mean you shouldn't make them.

2

The 5 Forces behind All Decisions and Why You Gravitate toward Some

When I first had the idea to write this book, I chuckled. Making a decision isn't that hard. You simply think about it and then decide. Who will ever buy a book on how to make better decisions? This was a few years ago, and here we are. The more I dug into it, the more I realized how complex decisions truly are. It's not far-fetched to say that our entire lives are shaped by the decisions we made. Some are banal, like our haircut, while others are life-changing, like choosing our romantic partner.

It became clear to me that we all intrinsically understood that we needed to make the right decisions. That part was obvious. What wasn't obvious was how to go about this and why we struggled with some decisions and not others. What are the elements that go into making a decision, and which one is the most important?

I'm skeptical of any situation where one element explains everything, and I don't think making better decisions comes down to just "one thing." However, I think that not everything has the same priority and weight, and the same applies to the elements of the decisions. I have organized these elements as follows:

1. 5 Driving Forces
2. Strategies
3. Problem-Solving
4. Turtleneck Principle
5. 3 Os
6. Intuitive

DOI: 10.4324/9781003185383-2

7. Ethics
8. Self-Analysis
9. Data

I also organized this book. An extra chapter applies these elements to unique situations like teams and companies, but this is what we will cover. This chapter covers the most important element, in my opinion, when it comes to decisions: driving forces. I call them the Hidden Currents behind all decisions. Once you learn about them, you will recognize them in your past and your future.

Driving forces are complicated. For example, take the first driving force: emotions. Sherlock Holmes famously rejected all emotions because they "clouded his thinking." Unlike Sherlock, we can't simply deny our emotions. That's not human work. I also think this is counterproductive since emotions aren't inherently negative. In the Buddhist world, it is said that "what you resist, persists." The same applies to the other four driving forces.

My list of the five driving forces are:

- Emotional
- Social
- Personal
- Intuitive
- Moral

Each of these driving forces will play an important role in our decisions. They might not be present in every single decision, but you will eventually come across them. Some of them deserve their own chapter, such as the Moral driving force. It's hard to properly cover this driving force in a couple of pages, let alone an entire book. People like Aristotle and Plato dedicated their entire lives to answering moral questions. My aim is to give you practical advice that you can use tomorrow (Figure 2.1).

I'll also start including the driving forces in the upcoming "Behind the Decision" sections and other anecdotes. You'll see how common they are once you start looking for them. I'll help you understand your primary driving force and how to minimize the bias (or force) that can come from each one. The driving forces push themselves against each other, making it harder to know the right choice.

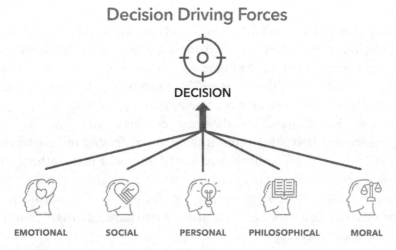

FIGURE 2.1
5 Driving forces behind decisions.

THE 5 DRIVING FORCES

Emotional

Let's start with the emotional driving force. This is the most straightforward one. Think back to a time when you made a decision while feeling angry or happy. The emotion colors your thinking, and it affects how you view options. Imagine someone who suffers through road rage. The moment they get cut off in traffic, accidentally or not, anger will take over. Their options for how to proceed will shift dramatically. Someone who is only mildly bothered will recognize that the person who cut them might have done this without knowing. The person with road rage will think it was personal and respond accordingly.

In the corporate world, we have all seen examples of emotions running wild. Elon Musk is a brilliant technologist and might just be on his way to change the world through companies like Tesla and SpaceX. Former employees have claimed that Elon has a huge ego that doesn't take criticism well. We have seen actions from him, as a CEO, that are baffling. This includes his meltdown on Twitter where he insulted the SEC or the time he insulted the British cave diver who helped save the Thailand children.

In these instances, it becomes clear that ego or another emotion is driving Elon to make rash decisions. Sometimes these decisions get him in trouble, like when the SEC fined him for inappropriate tweets. Sometimes, nothing happens to him except negative media coverage. We could accept that this is just "part of the brilliance" behind him, but this emotion could eventually get Elon in much more trouble than a slap on the wrist.

In your life, think about the most dominant emotions that you experience regularly. This could include anger, frustration, excitement, anxiety, dread, sadness, happiness, confidence, and many others. You might describe them using different words, and any given emotion could mean something different to you and me. The goal here is to identify the consistent emotional themes of our lives. We all have patterns of thinking that shape our everyday life.

Two emotions hold a special place and should be analyzed further: fear and overwhelm. Overwhelm is one of the most common emotions that I come across when working with clients. Executives are overwhelmed at everything that needs to get done, leading to 80-hour workweeks. Their teams are overwhelmed, leading to unforced errors and missed opportunities. I have personally felt overwhelmed with too much client work or responsibilities. This emotion affects all of us at some point in our lives.

Fear is what we feel whenever our lives are in danger. The moment before jumping off a plane when skydiving was full of fear for me. All I could see were the clouds and the rushing air being 12,000 feet up in the air. The first few seconds after jumping off the plane were exhilarating, and the fear was gone. Much has been written about fear in our modern life. We rarely come across situations that warrant fear, and yet we feel it regularly. We no longer feel fear because our life is threatened but because we perceive a risk that we can't quite articulate.

Both of these emotions share one attribute: the unknown. We feel overwhelmed because we aren't sure how we will get everything done. However, we don't always know what actually needs to get done and how much time it will take. The ambiguity around this causes overwhelms and paralysis. Likewise, we fear uncertainty because we can't fully control the future. No one knows what will happen in the future, which means we can imagine the worst possible scenarios.

Be mindful of these two emotions and similar ones. They distort our perception of how we should act and limit our decision-making. Instead of making logical choices, we start to weigh options based on the unknown. We turn down projects because we think we have too much on our plate or we avoid taking a new opportunity because of the fear of uncertainty. This is where the emotional driving force can lead us down the wrong path.

Once you identify your emotional driving force, run through the following questions to understand how this has affected decisions in the past:

- Would I have made a different decision if I had a different emotion? If you didn't feel overwhelmed but instead felt calm, would your decision have been different?
- How can I minimize negative emotions from affecting my decision-making?
- Are there any biases that I need to control in certain decisions? You may have a bias for action, but some decisions require deliberation.
- What emotions can I double down and use in more decisions?

Bias is an important point in the emotional driving force. I recently heard a podcast interview between Alan Weiss and Lisa Bing about race and racism.* Lisa made a fantastic point on how we should think about biases, prejudice, and racism. She defined each of these terms as follows:

- Biases: preferences we all have that range from ice cream choices to who we think is likely to succeed.
- Prejudice: when biases start affecting our behavior and how we interact with others. We may hire a candidate because they fit one of our biases.
- Racism: when we establish systemic rules based on our biases and prejudices.

This isn't a book about racism, but I think these definitions are helpful when understanding biases. We all have them. Over time, we might be able to change them, but some biases will never change. Instead, we should strive to become aware of them and learn how to hold them at bay in specific situations. Having a bias that MBAs are better suited for strategic

---

* "EPISODE 171: INTERVIEW WITH LISA BING," Alan Weiss, accessed January 19, 2021, https://alanweiss.com/interview-with-lisa-bing/

finance jobs isn't necessarily a bad thing. However, you should hold this bias back during interviews to avoid dismissing a candidate without an MBA degree. In essence, you're avoiding turning that bias into a prejudice when biases can become destructive.

Take the current political climate, especially in the United States. We see biases become prejudices in the strongest possible actions. In some cases, those prejudices might also become systemic racism. We see individuals who aren't just content with their worldviews; they hate anyone who believes otherwise: conservatives who hate liberals, liberals who hate conservatives. There is a strong emotional driving force behind these decisions, preventing them from making logical choices.

The political example is an extreme one, but you need to be mindful of the impact of your biases and what you're doing to propagate them or limit them. We interact with what we read, and what we consider success or failure all play a role in promoting our biases. You want to learn how to control your emotional driving force and use it for good instead of letting it drive you in whatever direction seems more convenient. Later on in this chapter, we'll look at how to double down on your primary driving force, and if that's emotional, you'll learn how to harness it for good.

Social

Our next driving force is Social. This is the driving force where we want to help others and do what is good for others. This is one of the strongest driving forces in not-for-profits and similar organizations. In this driving force, you'll put other ideas and needs aside if it means helping other people. You might even sacrifice your own needs as you put others first. Some cultures, such as Asian culture, are also driven by this driving force. The good of the community comes before the individual, and if you had a choice, you would choose the community.

We all have this driving force in some form. Humans are incredibly social, and almost everything that we do is social in some aspect. However, some of us are clearly driven by this force. Mother Teresa stands out as someone who was incredibly driven by the Social driving force. She spent her entire life helping others and even put herself in danger, such as when she rescued 37 children trapped in a hospital during the Siege of Beirut in

1982.* You need to have a high level of Social driving force to put yourself between two opposing armies.

In companies, you will also see the Social driving force in how executives manage their teams. All executives have different management styles, and some take a great interest in mentoring younger employees and helping them with their careers. I believe these executives have a high Social driving force, and they are willing to spend their lunch breaks and even time after work to guide someone through the right choices. They will even help employees find jobs elsewhere if their current job isn't a good fit for their personality and skills.

The Social driving force can be essential when building your team. You can't do things on your own, and one of the most common issues I see with executives is learning how to properly delegate and empower the people in their team. I was working with a mid-size company where the CEO was heavily involved in every decision, including relatively minor ones. He felt frustrated because these team members weren't taking the initiative in a new project and had to be guided through even the smallest of questions. The reality was there was no room for them to take ownership because the CEO overpowered everyone.

It wasn't his intention, but his Social driving force wasn't as strong. He felt comfortable making all the decisions and didn't quite know how to let go of the reins. This can happen at any company size but is especially challenging for companies going from "startup" to mature. In this transition, executives have to change from someone who can do everything to someone who can support the right people. Marshall Goldsmith's famous book, *What Got You Here Won't Get You There*, captures the essence of this transition in a few words.

When thinking of your Social force, take a moment to answer the following questions:

- How often do you think about others when making decisions?
- Do your decisions seem to lean toward what would make others happy while putting your own happiness last?

---

* "Mother Teresa, Patron of the World's Poorest, Dead at 87," SouthCoastToday, accessed January 20, 2021, https://www.southcoasttoday.com/article/19970906/News/309069981

- How much do you align with the idea of "helping others"?
- Are you ever concerned about what others will think of your decisions?

The Social driving force can sometimes play out in unusual ways. In 2020 and early 2021, we started to see certain stocks increase in value beyond any fundamentals. Gamestop (NYSE: GME) was one of the most well-known examples in this era. Gamestop is a company that sells video games through retail stores. It was struggling for years, and the COVID-19 pandemic put further pressure on its business. Consumers weren't buying as many physical games, and the company wasn't sure how to adjust. Despite consistent poor earnings, the stock rallied from around $20 at the end of December 2020 to around $350 by the end of January 2021.

This rally came through obscure parts of the internet that were encouraging each other to purchase it. Bloomberg News called it a "Rage Against the Financial Machine."* Amateur stock traders were buying the stock and pushing the price upwards. Professional hedge fund managers had short positions expecting the stock to crash down to its actual value, below $20. This was a battle of an online "mob" against Wall Street. Several hedge funds lost billions of dollars in their short positions, as they couldn't continue to hold them.

This situation is an example of how the Social driving force can unite people who don't even know each other to make the same decisions. There's also an element of anger and resentment (the emotional driving force) as these amateur traders take on Wall Street. It's unclear how this situation will end, but someone will lose money. They will get caught holding the bag of an overpriced stock once the frenzy ends. The SEC is also starting an investigation to understand if there are any regulatory laws being broken.

The Social driving force can also be forced. Dan Price of Gravity Payments, a small company in Seattle, decided that everyone should earn a minimum of $70,000 USD annually. As CEO, he had the complete power to make, and 70 of his 120 employees got a raise. Dan himself had to take a

---

* "GameStop Is Rage against the Financial Machine," Bloomberg, accessed January 20, 2021, https://www.bloomberg.com/opinion/articles/2021-01-27/gamestop-short-squeeze-is-rage-against-the-financial-machine

pay cut to make the numbers work. Productivity and employee happiness rose within the company in the years following.

Gravity Payments is a relatively small company, and these kinds of decisions might prevent them from growing into a billion-dollar company. All decisions have consequences, but as an executive, you have the freedom to make these choices. You can choose to build your team in certain ways or to sacrifice revenue in exchange for something else. Just be aware of the driving force behind these decisions, and make sure that it aligns with your personal and corporate goals.

One final example relates to how this driving force plays at the cultural level. If you have done any business internationally, you'll know that every culture has slightly different norms. The Japanese, for example, are known to be reserved, and there's a strong fear of shame. The wrong actions can lead to rejection from friends and colleagues. In Australia and New Zealand, you'll hear about the "tall poppy syndrome," where anyone who stands out too much will be "cut." In these two countries, you're expected to fit in and be part of society instead of simply being better than anyone else.

Personal

The third driving force is Personal or self-interest. Self-interest is a powerful force because it's our default position. We like making decisions that make us happy or that are enjoyable. This is obvious, but self-interest can be seen as "wrong." I think it is commonly mistaken for selfishness which is an excessive focus on ourselves. A mentor, Alan Weiss, has always talked about the "oxygen mask principle."* If you have ever flown, you're familiar with the security announcement at the beginning of every flight. There's a comment about putting your oxygen mask on first before helping others. This applies to everyone, even mothers who are traveling with their kids.

The "oxygen mask principle" tells us that everything in life is like this. You can't help others unless you help yourself first. If you are working yourself to death without taking proper care of yourself, you will eventually burn out. This is what can happen to many well-intentioned people in not-for-profit organizations. They are driven by their desire to help, and they

---

* "How to Stop Burnout with 1 Simple Rule," Inc., accessed January 22, 2021, https://www.inc.com/damon-brown/how-to-stop-burnout-with-one-simple-rule.html

put aside their own needs. They don't listen to their own Personal driving force.

In organizations, making a case for your team's self-interest is also a powerful way to get things done. When I work with clients, I'm trying to figure out what needs to happen and how to do it while appealing to the self-interest of my clients. Getting executives to delegate more becomes a way of helping the executive spend more time with their family and reduce their stress. The same can be applied to most situations within a company.

This will not be a surprise, but shaming or coercing people to do something isn't very effective. Think back to situations where you asked someone to take on a task, but it was done begrudgingly. This kind of work isn't as effective. Many words have been written about "buy-in" into a strategy or a culture. You can't force people to buy in; they need to come because they see a benefit to their self-interest. Shaming or coercing might get movement going, but it will be short-lived.

Cults understand this quite well. When they recruit new members, they do this by focusing exclusively on the person's self-interest. They may discover someone who is stressed out or struggling, and they offer help and support. Once the person is indoctrinated, they will switch to fear-based techniques to keep the person within their sphere of influence. Shame works quite well once the person has joined the cult, but people join cults because they believe there's something in it for them.

In decisions, we need to identify our Personal driving force. It's perfectly okay to make decisions that benefit us or that are exclusively in our self-interest. There's no law that states that we need to sacrifice and never experience joy or happiness. Well, perhaps some religions have laws that state this, but these are the exceptions. Be comfortable with making decisions for yourself, especially if this is not your norm. If you're only making decisions for yourself, you may need to balance this with the Social driving force.

Let me give you an example that affects many executives. As an executive, you will have quite a number of meetings. In fact, your entire day may just be back-to-back meetings. This makes it harder to do any deep thinking or tackle other aspects of your work. The solution to this is simple: block specific parts of your day or week. Even an hour or two will help give you back more control over your time. And yet, I get pushback to this idea. It's not possible, it's too hard, I just don't understand their specific situation.

Behind the technicalities, I see hesitation to make a decision based on your self-interest.

As you think about this driving force, ask yourself the following questions:

- When I make decisions, how much do I think about my own personal benefit?
- If I see someone making a decision that most benefits them, what do I think?
- Have other people told me that I need to do more things for myself, such as take a vacation or treat myself?
- Did you grow up in a culture where self-interest was shunned or actively repressed?

Doing things for our own benefit can be tricky, especially once we have other people we care for, such as children and older parents. Like everything in life, there's a balance to how much we should take care of ourselves and others. Any shift in this balance can lead to unusual situations or, worse, decisions that we end up regretting.

I also want to make a note about special kinds of decisions that merge the Personal and Social driving forces. This is when we take responsibility for others' decisions. I worked with an executive once who was quite talented but had a habit of picking up the slack from her team. If her team didn't do everything "correctly," she would go in and fix them. It was usually minor changes, but the outcome was devastating. Her team wasn't able to fail and learn because they had learned that they could rely on her to catch any missing elements.

We need to treat everyone as mature adults and stop internalizing their problems and challenges. I have personally struggled with this, as I sometimes get too emotionally involved in the challenges of my friends. In most situations, they are only looking for advice or someone to listen to their challenges, not solve them. By internalizing their problems, I'm simply making myself more stressed and not actually helping them. We all need the opportunity to work through challenges and learn from them. If anyone stops that, they can short circuit our problem-solving and resilience skills.

Be careful in confusing Social and Personal decisions. You may get satisfaction from helping others, but there's a balance between providing advice and a shoulder to lean on and actually doing things for them. Trust that the people around you, whether at work or in your personal life, are smart, resourceful, and able to figure out their toughest challenges. You can be there to guide them along the way, but you don't always need to solve the puzzle for them.

Intuitive

The fourth driving force is Intuitive. I love this driving force because it's under attack in our modern society. We live in a world driven by science, and things like intuition can be seen as "woo woo." Show me the facts, not how you think they can be commonly heard in offices worldwide. However, we shouldn't dismiss this driving force so easily. Our ability to find patterns and learn is unparalleled, even by the fastest computers. We are losing ground in some areas like chess and math, but there's a big gap between what robots can do and what our mind is capable of.

Let me give you some examples to show the power of our minds. As teenagers, one of the classic experiences of our lives is learning how to drive. An average teenager will learn how to drive a car in around 20 hours. This is enough time to drive in different conditions, at different times, and perhaps even learn how to drive manual (or stick). Once you go past these 20 hours, there's an incremental amount of driving knowledge. Perhaps you have never driven in snow, or you have never driven more than four hours at a time. Nonetheless, we can all reach an acceptable standard of driving within 20 hours.

Waymo, the self-driving company started by Google, has driven more than 20 million miles as of early 2020.* They have also "driven" tens of billions of miles through computer simulations, but we won't even include these. The Waymo self-driving project has been running for more than 11 years after it was started in 2009 within Google. It is considered one of the most advanced self-driving companies in the world and the most likely to actually get these cars on the road.

Despite this massive amount of driving, the cars aren't ready for consumers yet as of early 2021. Google has been doing full autonomous

---

* "Waymo's Autonomous Cars Have Driven 20 Million Miles on Public Roads," VentureBeat, accessed January 24, 2021, https://venturebeat.com/2020/01/06/waymos-autonomous-cars-have-driven-20-million-miles-on-public-roads/

testing in locations like Phoenix, where the weather is consistently sunny, but they have yet to tackle harsher climates like the winter in Michigan. Humans can learn how to drive in 20 hours, but machines need thousands of hours, and it is still unclear when they will be ready. Keep in mind that autonomous driving experiments have been around since the 1920s, and the first landmark cars came out in the 1980s. This is an old challenge that we have yet to crack.

I personally think we will see self-driving cars in my lifetime, but my point here is that we don't need to worry about machines taking over our jobs. There will always be things that we can do better, and intuition is one of them. In fact, I think one of the most valuable outcomes of using data is that we can train our intuition to be more accurate and reliable. It's not about abandoning intuition but finding a hybrid approach between technology and ourselves.

If you want to see the power of intuition, simply tune in to any sports channel. Intuition allows players to make plays that don't make statistical sense or that seem impossible. One of my favorite sites on the internet is FiveThirtyEight. Started by Nate Silver in 2008, it became famous due to the accuracy of its presidential forecast in the 2008 elections. It was eventually acquired by *The New York Times*, and it now covers the news through the lens of data. They have some of the best data journalism in the world, on par with what *The Economist* has been doing for over 100 years.

One of my gripes with their forecasts is around their prediction model for the NBA. They have built and rebuilt their models to try and predict the best players in the NBA and the team most likely to win the championship. The models are incredibly complex, and they update as the season progresses. As a huge fan of LeBron James, I'm typically biased against any model that doesn't rank him as highly as it should. He often overperforms their model, as LeBron is known to increase his impact during the playoffs while "coasting" through the regular season.

Let's take a look at their prediction model for 2019–2020.* At the beginning of the season, the four teams most likely to win the NBA championship were the Houston Rockets, Philadelphia 76ers, LA Lakers, and the Golden State Warriors. The actual final two teams were the Lakers and the Miami Heat. The Lakers, where LeBron plays, went on to win

---

* "2019-20 NBA Predictions," FiveThirtyEight, accessed January 28, 2021, https://projects.fivethir tyeight.com/2020-nba-predictions/

the championship. The Miami Heat had a 4% chance of even making the finals, according to the model. Granted, this season was cut short due to COVID-19, and they had to continue playing through the NBA bubble in Walt Disney World. Facts don't always tell the full story.

I'm not saying that we should dismiss these kinds of models. Just as this example didn't fully predict the outcome, we can find models that are quite accurate. We see this a lot in finance, where software and machine learning are changing how hedge funds approach investing. They are able to use software to process large volumes of data and combine that with the soft knowledge of traders to make even better decisions. This goes back to my example of using data to improve your intuition instead of trying to replace it altogether.

As you think about this driving force, ask yourself the following questions:

- How often do you know the right answer but can't explain how you arrived there?
- Do you dismiss intuition, or do you try to harness it?
- Has your intuition gotten better or worse as you got older?
- Are there specific areas where your intuition has worked well? On the flip side, are there areas where your intuition hasn't worked as well?

Executives are surrounded by decisions where intuition is the perfect fit. You're trying to hire the right candidate for your team, or you're trying to determine if it makes sense to go into a multi-year partnership with another company. You have all the facts, you did all the interviews, and you're left with the final decision. How does this feel to you? Do you get an uneasy feeling, or are you excited? Is this decision obvious, or is there uncertainty that prevents you from pulling the trigger?

You wouldn't want to make every single decision based on intuition. There's a reason why we need to build up our ability to think critically, problem-solve, and weigh the evidence. Juries are told that they need to objectively approach the evidence. It's common to ask juries to dismiss testimony they just heard because it isn't relevant to the case. In some cases, there are even attempts to prevent the juries from watching the news to avoid being swayed away from the evidence. This is, of course, quite hard, but it is part of our justice system.

In your life, think about the role intuition has played and what role you want it to play in the next few years. I think there are multiple ways to build this driving force and use it in the appropriate situations. We'll talk more about how to balance this raw energy with intellectual safeguards in future chapters.

Moral

The fifth driving force is Moral. This is the most complicated force because of its inherent complexity. We are all familiar with morality and ethics, but we all define them slightly differently. It's easy to agree on major questions such as murder, but it gets much harder on the smaller things. Is it ethical to take your coworkers to lunch and claim it as a business expense? If you have the option to fly business class but decide to fly coach, should you keep the difference? Should you use data about competitors to inform your strategy?

Take the example of interpersonal relationships. McDonald's, one of the best-run companies, has run into ethical challenges in the past few years. Its previous CEO, Steve Easterbrook, was fired in 2019 for violating company policy and engaging in a relationship with an employee.* This wasn't the end of it though. In 2020, McDonald's sued Easterbrook because he allegedly concealed evidence about the nature of his relationships. McDonald's wanted to recover the $40 million severance package he received. Allegedly, Steve had relationships with at least three women and even awarded stock options to one of them. The lawsuit is ongoing as of early 2021.

Let's break this down. Company policy states that no interpersonal relationship should take place between co-workers, especially for executives like the CEO. From the beginning, this would put Steve in the wrong, but is it ethically inappropriate? This is where things get complex. If the relationships were consensual, then there could be an ethical argument for it. The case gets more complicated since we suspect there were multiple relationships and even stock options awarded. I think you could easily find someone who thinks this behavior is wrong, and you

---

* "McDonald's Sues to Recover Severance from Fired CEO, Claiming He Lied about Affairs with Employees," *Wall Street Journal*, accessed January 28, 2021, https://www.wsj.com/articles/mcdona lds-sues-to-recover-severance-from-fired-ceo-claiming-he-lied-about-affairs-with-employees-11597064924

might also find people who think the behavior broke the company rules but isn't unethical.

How do you sort through these murky waters? We need to start by defining terms. Language is everything, and many disagreements could be solved by agreeing on the same definitions. For this book, I will talk about morality as a set of principles that governs what is right and wrong. We may disagree on these principles, but I will do my best to apply them consistently. In your life, you also need to do the same. Is your team clear on what is acceptable and what isn't? Where should people draw the line?

Don't assume that everyone is on the same page. You may consider spying on competitors to be morally wrong and unacceptable, but others may not. In your teams, run through the following questions:

- What is morally acceptable and unacceptable to you?
- If you had the opportunity to peek into a competitor's strategy without any repercussions, would you do it?
- What current company rules do you think are unnecessary?

You can run through these questions in a workshop format, and you should also provide opportunities for people to provide anonymous feedback. High-level questions are good starting points, but you eventually want to talk about actual situations within your company. Company expenses, studying competitors, interpersonal relationships, and feedback are hot areas for any team. Your goal is to establish clear rules for how your team should operate. At the end of the day, what people do under your circumstances represents your beliefs.

An example of questionable moral principles is Uber. I'll be the first to admit that the company provides a superior experience to taxis, and I was glad when they eventually came to Vancouver in 2020. However, the company's incredible growth was done through shady means. Uber's initial strategy was to start operating within a city without complying with regulations. If and when caught, they launched local political campaigns and asked their users to lobby local politicians. This led Uber to fight regulations all over the world.

Travis Kalanick was the original proponent of this "win at all costs" mentality.* Uber has all been caught trying to poach drivers from other

---

* "'He Wants to Be a Cool Startup Founder,'" Slate, accessed February 1, 2021, https://slate.com/te chnology/2019/09/uber-travis-kalanick-silicon-valley-mike-isaac-if-then.html

services such as Lyft. There are even cases of Uber employees spamming competitor services with fake orders in the hope of overwhelming them. Finally, Uber created a special software called Greyball used to deny service to special users. This software was used to prevent local authorities from getting on Ubers and slow down any active investigations.

The list of ethically questionable things that Uber has done is endless. It's no surprise that it was hit with sexual harassment lawsuits left and right. The culture that Travis and other executives created led to many of these decisions. The moral principles of a company can manifest in unexpected ways. I'm not sure if any executive ever said, "we should spam our competitors" or "we shouldn't let any government official hail an Uber." The moral principles embodied by leadership then allow employees to determine if their actions will be congruent with what the company believes.

Uber is changing. In 2017, Travis Kalanick resigned as CEO, and in 2019, he resigned from the board of directors. Dara Khosrowshahi is now in charge of culture and doing his best to clean up all the mess. It's not an easy job, especially after years of hearing the same messages over and over again. For now, it seems like Uber is doing a better job at making the correct moral decisions while still keeping the interests of shareholders in mind.

The tricky thing about the Moral driving force is that we only become aware of it when it goes horribly wrong, like in the examples of Uber and the McDonald's CEO. The majority of companies operate within good moral principles, but those stories don't usually make the news. Determine the appropriate moral code for your team and then work to enforce it. Remember that people pay attention to actions and not words. Don't focus so much on what is written on the walls and instead focus on what is happening in the hallways.

BEHIND THE DECISION: THE ASTROS SIGN STEALING OPERATION

In 2017, the Houston Astros won the baseball World Series, their first championship in franchise history. The team, fans, and community were elated. They lost in the playoffs in 2018, but they were back in the World

Series in 2019, which they lost. Overall, it was not a bad three years, as any baseball team would love to be in the World Series twice and win at least once.

In early 2020, the mood changed in Houston after MLB announced that they were suspending the Astros manager, A.J. Hinch, and general manager Jeff Luhnow for one year after an investigation discovered a widespread sign-stealing operation during the 2017 and 2018 season. Eventually, both of these men were fired from the team. The team was also fined $5 million dollars, and gave up their 2020 and 2021 picks.[*]

If you're not familiar with baseball and sign stealing, here's what you need to know. When a batter is up on the plate, the catcher will provide signs for how the pitcher should throw the ball. Sometimes these signs can come from the coach or other players in the dugout. The batter can't see these signs since they typically happen behind his back.

There's no law that prohibits a team from trying to intercept these signals, and they could be a source of an unfair advantage. If you know what type of ball the pitcher will throw, you may be more likely to actually hit it. Nevertheless, the Astros were caught stealing their opponent's signals through an elaborate computer system in their home field. They then provided a sound to warn their batters of what type of pitch was coming.

Every team in baseball wants to win, and they are looking for the edge that will get them. Some find them in unconventional methods like the Oakland Athletics, which looked for other attributes in players as depicted in *Moneyball*, the book, and film. It seems the Astros took advantage of the fact that sign stealing was not illegal and created an elaborate technical system.

In our framework, we know that the outcome was to win the World Series. They looked through all the options and decided on the sign-stealing one. They also had to play good baseball, and I don't want to make it seem like stealing signs was the key reason they won in 2017. They also worked through all the obstacles, including the technical details of their system and training their batters to recognize the relevant sounds.

In the end, the Astros won the 2017 World Series, and we could conclude that the sign stealing was worth it. The fines and firing hurt but are

---

[*] "Everything You Need to Know about MLB's Sign-Stealing Scandal," Slate, accessed February 3, 2021, https://www.espn.com/mlb/story/_/id/28476282/everything-need-know-mlb-sign-stealing-scandal

likely temporary setbacks for them. However, the 2017 World Series now has an asterisk next to it, and anyone could simply say that the Astros won because of cheating. I think it would be hard to find someone who could claim otherwise.

DOUBLING DOWN ON YOUR PRIMARY FORCE

As mentioned at the beginning of this chapter, we all have a primary driving force. Some of us are driven by the Social force, constantly thinking of the good of others. Others have a strong intuition that guides them through all of their decisions. We don't want to go deeply against our nature. As the famous phrase goes, we need to build on strengths and not weaknesses. The goal is to supplement your driving force and not outright replace it.

The first step is to recognize the force behind the majority of your decisions. This doesn't mean that every decision you make will be based on the same force, but one tends to come up more often than the others. You can recognize by running the questions in previous sections and gauging how well your answers align with the theory of each force. You can also think about the most important decisions that you have made recently and analyze them through the lens of each driving force. Was that a Social or Personal driven decision?

The second step is to understand the blind spots behind each driving force. We talked about how Social-driven decisions can leave you feeling frustrated and resentful if you never do something for yourself. Morally wrong decisions can lead to disaster, as seen in the Uber example. Make a note of all the different ways this force has affected the outcomes of your decisions. This is much easier to do in hindsight, and after all the energy has subsided.

The third step is to find another driving force that could complement the gaps that you're seeing. Some forces align well with each other such as the Social and Personal forces. However, you need to determine in what ways you wish decisions had turned out differently. What would you have said if you could go back in time? What issues would try to prevent it with the full power of hindsight?

You can see this play out in the COVID-19 pandemic. Soon into the pandemic, we realized that lockdowns were having a significant impact on most people's mental health. I myself felt the stress of the COVID-19 in the earlier months of 2020. As the pandemic wore on, it became clear to me that some people were making decisions exclusively based on one force. You had a group of people who lived under total lockdown despite no need for this. They were young and didn't interact with high-risk individuals.

This group of people became resentful of other people breaking restrictions. You might remember the uproar when it was discovered that some people were traveling. This isn't to say that traveling was right, but I think these people could have made themselves feel better by balancing their Social force with a Personal force. They could have realized that they could go for walks with friends, eat out, or do other activities within their local restrictions.

On the corporate side, I think we saw a balance of multiple forces when Jeff Bezos decided to step down as CEO of Amazon in early 2021. By this point, Jeff wasn't actually as involved in the day-to-day operations of Amazon, but his official stepping down was still a milestone for the company. Amazon was coming off an incredible growth period through the COVID-19 pandemic. The stock was up, earnings were up, and everything looked good.

At this point, Jeff decided to balance his Emotional, Personal, and Social driving forces. He left at the top of his game within Amazon because it was the right thing for the company. His successor can take over a successful company instead of trying to revive a dying business, as we have seen in other situations. I don't think it was easy for Jeff to leave the company that he spent 30 years building and to do it at the time that he did.

In your situation, think about the power of having multiple forces guide your decisions. You can start to cover your blind spots instead of living with them. Unlike in a car, personal blind spots can be put under the correct light once you adopt different decision-making driving forces. It might take some time to get used to it, but the result is worth it.

BEHIND THE DECISION: LEBRON JAMES AND "THE DECISION"

I love basketball, but I don't follow a specific team. I live in Vancouver, Canada, so we don't actually have an NBA team. I follow LeBron James, and I usually cheer for whatever team he plays on. LeBron is a generational player who continues to amaze. At 36 years old, he's still a top five player in the league, showing no signs of slowing down. Watching him feels like what I imagine watching Michael Jordan was like in the 1990s. This "Behind the Decision" isn't about how he plays the game, though. It's actually about one of the most controversial events in LeBron's career, aptly called "The Decision."*

Let's start with some context. LeBron was drafted by the Cleveland Cavaliers, which was convenient since he was born in Akron, Ohio. He played seven seasons with the Cavaliers and failed to win a championship. This wasn't unusual, but rumors started that LeBron wanted to change teams in the hopes of winning his first championship. LeBron James has been one of the most hyped NBA drafts in recent history, and he was able to live up to the hype. In the 2010 offseason, he was the most valuable free agent on the market.

Free agency is usually negotiated between agents and teams. Rumors swirl for weeks and months, but the deals are done in private. LeBron, or his team, were convinced that there was a business opportunity in his free agency. They decided to host a one-hour TV special where LeBron James would announce what team he would be playing for in the fall of 2010. ESPN gladly paid for the rights, and the interview took place despite the NBA's wishes.

The special, "The Decision," ran for 75 minutes on July 8, 2010. Halfway through the show, LeBron announced that he would be "taking his talents to South Beach and join the Miami Heat." I also have to note that the show was also an opportunity to raise $2.5 million for Connecticut's Boys and Girls Club. The show also donated an additional $3.5 million from the advertisement revenue. Around 10 million people watched the show, and while it seemed like a good idea at the beginning, it quickly gathered criticism in the days the followed.

It turns out that the Cavaliers, James's current team, was informed of his decision to join Miami minutes before the show aired. Miami, of course, knew ahead of time as they needed to hash the details of the contract and expectations. Fans were upset and even proceeded to burn his shirts. They felt it was a betrayal, and perhaps one

---

* "Looking Back at LeBron's Decision 10 Years Later," SI, accessed February 6, 2021, https://www.si.com/nba/2020/07/08/lebron-james-miami-heat-decision-10-years-later

made into a bigger deal through the show. The Cavaliers owner, Dan Gilbert, wrote a public letter denouncing James's decision. This letter would be famous since it was written in Comic Sans, which made it harder to take seriously.

LeBron leaving Cleveland was already a controversial decision. Everyone had an opinion on it, and the impact of this decision was made worse through the show. Players like LeBron have every right to play wherever they want. It's their talent on the court every night, and they aren't the property of any NBA team. However, the public format of this decision ended up backfiring for LeBron. He went on to win two championships with the Miami Heat, and he came back to the Cavaliers in 2014. When he came back home, he skipped the press conference and simply wrote a letter for *Sports Illustrated*. The Cavaliers would win their first NBA championship in 2016 with James, their first sports title in 52 years.

In this scenario, we see a potentially good idea go sideways. LeBron James and everyone involved didn't fully take into account how people would feel about the show and him leaving the Cavaliers. To make the show work, almost everyone had to be kept in the dark, which led to frustration leading up to the show. Finally, it was an unusual way of dealing with something that happens all the time. Players leave teams regularly, but it's just business. "The Decision" turned this routine move into something special.

The lessons here come down to the repercussions of our decisions. If there's a decision that could have implications for our public image, we need to consider those effects. This was true 100 years ago, and is even more true now in the world of social media. Our decisions will get interpreted in many ways, and while we will always find critics, there's no need to give them more ammo than is needed by choosing a grandiose or unnecessary option.

MINIMIZING THE BIAS GENERATED BY EACH FORCE

The last thing I want to talk about is how to minimize the bias generated by each force. I recently moved apartments from one built in the 1970s to one built in 2015. Forty-five years have made a big difference in building standards, but the thing that surprised me the most about the new apartment was how quiet it was. I was even more surprised since the new building was closer to the core of Vancouver downtown, and there's significantly more traffic and noise around it.

The secret to this is, of course, the construction. The apartment uses modern windows which have multiple glass panels, and even the walls themselves are better designed to block out sound. To maintain a proper seal, the apartment also has central heating, which can keep the apartment warm or cool without having to open the windows often. I'm still amazed every time I sit down to eat or watch TV.

These same ideas can be applied to your decision-making driving force. Each force will generate bias or noise. The Social force makes you choose decisions that benefit the group over decisions that don't. If you come across a situation that doesn't require group benefits, you could go down the wrong path. You need to find ways to make decisions in a quiet environment where these biases are blocked out. I spoke briefly about biases above, but I want to dive deeper in this final section.

When making an important decision, start by thinking about the ideal force for this decision. If you need to make a decision that will affect your team, the Social force would be the best choice. If you need to decide where you have little data, you can use the Intuitive force. The outcome that you're trying to achieve will help you sort through the five options. Over time, you will also get a sense as to what force is most relevant in different situations.

Next, think about what issues you could encounter with this decision. We'll talk more about problem-solving and other situations but for now, simply think about the different ways in which this decision could unravel. If you're hiring a new team member, think about the different possibilities such as:

- The team member performs above expectations.
- The team member performs great in some areas and ok in others.
- The team member performs below expectations.

Based on these outcomes, you can then start to think about how each force might play a role in the decision. Perhaps you have a bias toward people with multiple degrees, or you're eager to finish this hiring, leading you to rush the process. You won't catch all the possibilities, and the toughest blind spots can sometimes only be tackled with an external coach, but this is a good starting point.

Make sure to minimize external influences, especially in the final stages. There are all kinds of external influences that can affect us such as the news, colleagues, our bosses, spouses, and friends. Influences can be positive, negative, or neutral, and they can be helpful at certain stages in the decision-making process. However, we don't want to use them as crutches or get them to make the decisions worse. The goal here is to get comfortable working through all the information and make a decision.

Find a literal quiet spot. In my apartment example, I talk about quietness. You should also seek out quiet locations where you can process through all the information and different forces. You may go for a walk in nature or retreat to a specific room in your house. We live in a world full of stimuli, and sometimes all we need is a few minutes to think without any distractions or influences. Regardless of how you achieve this, this can be an instrumental part, especially when dealing with your toughest decisions.

CHAPTER SUMMARY

- There are five driving forces behind decisions: Emotional, Social, Personal, Intuitive and Moral.
- The Emotional driving force leads when we make decisions due to anger or excitement.
- The Social driving force leads when we make decisions based on what's best for the group.
- The Personal driving force leads when we make decisions based on our own self-interest.
- The Intuitive driving force leads when we rely on our gut to make decisions.
- The Moral driving force leads the underlying set of principles in which we make decisions.
- Build on success by doubling down on your primary driving force.
- Learn how to minimize the force generated by thinking through all the information in a quiet environment and minimizing external influences.

3

Before You Decide, Choose a Problem Worth Solving

There's something special about solving problems, especially one that has been plaguing us for months or years. We are problem-solving machines at our core. Self-development books love to talk about how humans behaved thousands of years ago and how these behaviors are still present in us today. I'm skeptical of making too many connections, but I can safely say that our ability and desire to problem-solve have been around for a long time.

In the past, we found ways to solve our lack of food or protect ourselves from predators and the environment. We solved organizational issues and eventually developed ways of growing food without having to hunt. We then created machines to do it for us and continue to solve our most pressing problems. History is a series of events where we solve a problem. Malaria, check. Polio, check. Slow internet, mostly check.

This desire to problem-solve is so strong that we will start doing it unconsciously. Men are notorious for doing this. The classic story that you hear is that men will try to solve the problems of women. A man can't simply listen to someone talk about a problem; he needs to provide solutions and next steps. Sometimes, people just want to be listened to. This doesn't mean that women don't fall prey to the same instincts, as I have met many female executives who are incredibly prone to problem-solving, and that's their biggest challenge.

In this chapter, I want to talk about the most effective ways to diagnose and solve problems. I also want to help you avoid getting stuck in problem-solving mode. At some point, you know what the problem is, and you need

DOI: 10.4324/9781003185383-3

to make a decision. Problem-solving is a means to an end, and in this book, the end is making decisions. We want to be good enough at solving problems, but we also want to be great at making the right decisions when the time is right.

This is also the first strategy in dealing with overwhelm. There's a large amount of energy that is spent tackling the wrong problems. Just because something isn't working doesn't mean that it should be fixed. Companies and our lives can be complex. Things may never feel "perfect," but that doesn't mean that we need to solve every little annoyance. This strategy aims to determine if a problem is worth solving and, if so, how to quickly diagnose the cause. Once we know the cause, then we can determine what decision to make.

IS THIS A PROBLEM WORTH SOLVING?

A problem isn't intrinsically worth solving merely by its existence. This can be hard to accept, but we need to focus on things that are worth solving. Whenever you come across a problem, you have two choices: solve it or ignore it. We will focus on solving this chapter, but it's just as important to know when you should ignore a problem. Ignoring a problem doesn't mean that you have to live with it. Some problems will actually disappear on their own accord and without any active intervention.

Learning how to find problems worth solving isn't just a question of prioritization. It also involves critical thinking to understand the potential implications of solutions. I have a client who is constantly in reactive mode when it comes to marketing campaigns. They are always looking for ways to improve their existing campaigns by a few percentage points, but they aren't moving the revenue needle. In their situation, they are too focused on the micro problems instead of solving the macro ones, such as strategy and focus resources.

This kind of microfocus can become quicksand. There's an emotional reward that we get from solving problems regardless of how small they are. I'm not a handyman, but I feel satisfied when I replace a lightbulb that burned out or figured out the solution to a client's problem. The scale of these two situations can be wildly different, but my emotional response is quite similar. They are just problems that need a solution. The client I mentioned above is looking to solve any problem instead of putting their limited effort into the right ones.

This micro-focus can also be hard to get out of. This is especially true for organizations that are really good at execution. There are always things to do and deadlines to hit, so they can get stuck in execution mode without any conscious effort. There's a reason why weekend retreats have become more popular in recent times. It's rare to get enough time to think through what is happening and whether you're spending your time correctly.

Companies that lose this macro focus can end up in trouble. When the first iPhone came out in 2006, the executives at Blackberry were shocked.* On the one hand, they were amazed at the technology, but on the other hand, they were the dominant player in the market. They didn't know how to compete with the phone, and the next few years were spent trying to solve the micro problems of building a touchscreen, building an app store, etc.

In the end, Blackberry lost its dominant position and would have been better off trying to solve the macro problem of their strategy instead of trying to solve every micro problem. This is what we have seen Blackberry do in recent years as they have shifted to secure enterprise communications. They had great strength in keeping communications secure through BBM and their email, but they didn't know how to build modern touchscreen phones. Realizing this ten years ago would have been helpful.

To get out of the microfocus, you need something that will take out the minutia. Start with the overall strategy of the company and your role in it. You may be the executive in charge of marketing or the executive in sales. Your goal is to solve the problems of aligning with the overall strategy and figuring out the big pieces that need to come together. You're effectively setting the parameters for how people under you should operate and what problems they need to solve.

Jeff Bezos from Amazon was famous for setting parameters for Amazon. He often talked about making three good decisions per day[†] and banning Powerpoint from meetings. Instead, he asked people to prepare briefing memos that would be read in silence at the start of the meeting. These

---

* "The Inside Story of How the iPhone Crippled BlackBerry," *Wall Street Journal*, accessed February 13, 2021, https://www.wsj.com/articles/behind-the-rise-and-fall-of-blackberry-1432311912

† "Jeff Bezos Only Expects Himself to Make Three Good Decisions a Day," Quartz, accessed February 16, 2021, https://qz.com/work/1390844/jeff-bezos-only-expects-himself-to-make-three-good-decisions-a-day/

memos are usually a few pages long and take 15–30 minutes to read. The rest of the meeting is then used to discuss the ideas and points in the memo.

You may not agree with all the decisions Jeff made, but you can't deny that these specific parameters make it easier for people to know what is expected of them. The downside of the memo approach from Amazon is that people now obsess over the contents of this document, and there are reports of people spending days and weeks refining the memo. You may now have too much time spent on one document.

To understand if a problem is worth solving, answer the following questions:

- What is the problem?
- What is the root cause of the problem?
- Do I care about this problem?

This is problem-solving 101, and many books have been written about this topic. Two of my favorites are *The Art of Problem Solving* by Russell Ackoff and *The New Rational Manager* by Benjamin Tregoe and Charles Kepner. You'll find that the ideas in this chapter overlap with these two books.

Getting better at this process can pay huge dividends. Take the recent news that Mercedes Benz is splitting from Daimler.* They merged back in 1926 and decided to split into two companies in 2021. The executives realized customers who buy a Mercedes car are quite different from those who buy Daimler trucks. The former focus on features, look, and brand, while the latter focus on costs and performance.

Think of the problem-solving that had to take place to get to this decision. The executive team had to realize that there was more potential as separate companies than one. They had to run through the analysis of the split and then determine a plan for doing so. So far, it's looking like the right decision.

---

* "Daimler to Separate Its Trucks Business from Mercedes-Benz Cars," *Wall Street Journal*, accessed February 19, 2021, https://www.wsj.com/articles/daimler-to-split-mercedes-benz-daimler-trucks-into-separate-companies-11612369055

BEHIND THE DECISION: CUBA AND COMMUNISM

In 1953, Fidel Castro, Che Guevara, and other guerillas led a revolution that toppled the Cuban government and established a communist regime. Cuba aligned with the Soviet Union and inadvertently joined the global Cold War of the 20th century. Seventy years later, Cuba is one for the few countries in the world that still lives under communism.

Cuba before Castro took over was fascinating. It was run by a corrupt government led by Fulgencio Batista, who took total government control in a 1952 coup. The Cuban economy under Batista did flourish, and Cuba was considered one of the five most developed countries in Latin America by the time Castro took over. Cuba also had a strong medical system, low mortality rates, and high literacy rates.

So why did Castro feel the need to topple the Batista government? Despite the corruption, Cuba seems to perform well against its peers in Latin America. The issue was that Batista became more dictatorial as time progressed. The economy wasn't growing as quickly in the 1950s as it did in the 1940s. Batista also formed alliances with the Mafia and started exploiting Cuban resources.

Castro tried to win political support, but Batista suspended the 1952 elections, taking full government control. This was when Castro decided to start a revolution and take control by force. The fighting lasted from 1953 to 1959 until Batista fled the country and Castro took control.

It seems to me that Castro assumed that the problems plaguing Cuba were related to Batista. If he could be removed, then Cuba's problems would be solved. Interestingly enough, Castro doesn't appear to be a communist and instead focused on opposing Batista and the United States, who supported Batista.

After Castro took over, he established himself as a dictator and fully embraced communism. Cuba's economy has struggled ever since, and rations are extremely common. Lack of food, electricity, and other supplies are in short supply on the island. Cuba never recovered to the pre-Castro position.

In hindsight, we can see that Castro was right in identifying the root cause issue of Cuba, but he made the wrong decision when determining the solution. Embracing communism and cutting themselves from the United States, their closest trade partner, would hurt them for years. Even today, the Cuban government is unable to reverse the decisions made in the 1950s.

EFFECTIVE PROBLEM-SOLVING IS GOOD CRITICAL THINKING

Let's build on the three questions from the last section. A common pitfall is to rush through the answers and end up going down the wrong street. Each question has a critical piece of the puzzle in your problem-solving arsenal.

What is the problem?

We need to start by understanding what the problem is. I worked with a client who was dealing with sales problems. Their sales teams weren't converting enough leads, and they were trying to understand what could be going wrong. After spending some time with the sales and marketing team, I determined that the problem wasn't the sales reps but the quality of the leads.

They could move heaven and earth, but their success would be limited because they were tackling the wrong problem. Better yet, fixing the quality of the leads was easier than reinventing their sales process to find improvements. This would also help with customer support since they also saw refunds from customers who weren't ready to buy.

Ben Tregoe calls this the "Problem Statement," and it simply specifies what the problem is. It also specifies what the problem isn't. This is a problem with the quality of the leads and not a problem with the sales process. As the first question, it will then guide your efforts in questions two and three.

The best process for understanding and refining your problem statement comes from *The New Rational Manager* book. The book walks you through an exercise of establishing what the problem is and isn't. It looks at four dimensions: what, where, when, and extent. The what is the lead quality, the where is affecting all the sales reps, the when is something that has been taking place for years, and the extent is affecting the entire sales team.

As you can see, problem-solving is a process of elimination and critical thinking. If a problem has been around for years, it isn't the fault of the newly hired Head of Sales. If a problem affects all the reps equally, then it isn't a specific rep. We can determine what the actual problem is by eliminating what isn't. In the example above, I was skeptical that an entire sales team could be underperforming, especially when they seemed to be doing the right things.

What is the root cause of the problem?

Once we know the problem, we can move on to determining the root cause. In reality, you will likely go back and forth between looking for the root cause and determining the problem as these trains of thought overlap with each other. Nonetheless, we need to find the true root cause of a problem before taking any action. This is especially important when dealing with people-related issues where someone could be laid off or affected.

Let's go back to COVID-19. We know the virus isn't deadly for the majority of people, though mortality varies from country to country. We also know that there's a population that is severely affected by the virus, and we need to protect them. The problem is governments tend to choose the most expensive option possible: lockdowns. By staying home, you guarantee that there will be no spread of the virus, but that isn't the only way to accomplish that.

Imagine that testing for the virus could be done quickly and effectively. We are just starting to see 15 minute at-home COVID-19 tests that could be purchased in bulk and mailed out. If you could test negative, you could proceed to your normal activities. People could carry cards or apps that state the status of their last test. Major businesses like airports could test individuals and hold them for a few minutes while the results are processed.

Developing this kind of testing infrastructure isn't easy. I have seen some private companies that now offer this service, but there isn't enough supply. However, the point of this example is that the root cause of the COVID-19 problem is that we can't know when we are carrying the virus. Since we can't do that rapidly, we have forced ourselves into lockdown as the next best option.

After defining the problem, we need to find the root cause. We don't want to cut a tree and leave the stump. We want to get the roots out of the ground to prevent any issues in the future. Determine the root cause by going through the chain of events that got you here. You may be dealing with a sales issue, but you want to go up the chain to see if there's something that happened before this moment that had an impact on what you're seeing.

Do I care about this problem?

After stating the problem and finding the root cause, you need to determine if you care about this problem. It sounds like a silly question, but not all problems need resolutions. Some problems may resolve on their own accord, and others are things you can live with. Your business may have a high churn rate, but that's expected as your company is in the middle of changing strategies and who you work with. This is a problem that you won't care about right now.

Team issues can fall in this category as well. You may have people in your teams that don't like each other, but they still can perform at a high level. You may know the problem and the root cause, but it's not something you need to fix. Unless you're running an employment agency or a summer camp, your job isn't to help your team members make new friends.

Answering these three questions will help you narrow down the number of problems that you need to tackle. It's the first strategy in this book because we need to spend our limited time and energy on the right things. You may be running very fast, but you won't go anywhere if you're on a treadmill. Internalizing good problem-solving skills is a fundamental skill for yourself and your team.

I don't think the process of problem-solving is complex. You could learn it in an hour and then internalize it after using it a few times. The challenge is that we can add emotion and biases into the process. An external person can see things clearly because they aren't emotionally invested, but it's much harder to do that with our own problems.

If you're assigned the sales process problem from above, and you have a history of bumping heads with the sales team, it might be harder to consider that this isn't a sales problem at all. The bias seeps and prevents you from seeing what is actually happening without any attachment to the outcome. This is the reason why people like me have jobs. I can come in and see a problem-free from the history, politics, and culture of a company.

There's also a history associated with most problems. Take the way we manage economies now—economic theory used to be built heavily on the idea of managing the interest. Central banks would focus on this number and aim to keep it at an acceptable level, typically around 2%. Suddenly, interest rates kept dropping, and now see negative interest in places like Europe. Negative interest rates weren't even a possibility in economic theory in the last 50 years, and now they are a reality.

Central banks now use QE (Qualitative Easing) to manage the economy. QE is when a central bank buys bonds directly to inject money while still keeping inflation steady. The history of how economies used to be managed still hangs over analysts, government officials, and citizens. You see this as an obsession over a country's debt. However, in a world with low-interest rates, debt isn't that important.

We may see a reversion back to the economic ideas of the 70s, or this may be the new normal. Either way, central banks need to adjust how they view the economy and then decide based on the new paradigm. The history of an idea or team can weigh heavily when problem-solving. The past isn't an indication of the future, but it is more real since we actually lived through it.

Take a moment to think back to a pivotal problem that you solved successfully. How did you think about these three questions, whether consciously or unconsciously? Did you follow a similar sequence, or did you jump around? In my experience, people who are incredibly good at problem-solving tend to follow a similar pattern in their minds. They might not expose it through writing, but it is happening in their minds.

Now do the opposite and think about a problem that you just couldn't seem to solve. Perhaps you tried different ideas, but none of them stick. What was different about this problem, and how did you approach it? A common pitfall when dealing with problems is that we try to solve them too fast. This is counterintuitive, but there is such a thing as rushing through problem-solving.

OCCAM'S RAZOR AND WHY A STRAIGHT LINE IS THE SHORTEST PATH

Occam's Razor is a popular idea in our culture that tells us that we should choose the simplest one if we are selecting among multiple explanations. The goal isn't to make things simple but to choose options or causes that involve fewer assumptions. The more assumptions or moving parts something has, the more complex and unlikely it will be.

My favorite example of Occam's Razor is conspiracy theories. If you have read anything about conspiracy theories, you'll realize that they are incredibly intricate. It involves multiple groups of people collaborating for a long time and aiming toward a huge goal like world domination. These theories tend to also combine conflicting ideas. On the one hand, governments have withheld secrets for hundreds of years, but on the other hand, governments are incompetent, and they can't be trusted.

Most conspiracy theories fail Occam's Razor theory because for the theory to work, you need multiple assumptions to work perfectly. The conspiracy theories that have been proven right in recent times tend to be some of the simplest such as the MKUltra research program. Beyond conspiracy theories, Occam's Razor is essential in our problem-solving process. We are looking for the cause of the problem with the fewest assumptions that is most likely to be true.

This doesn't mean that we will attach ourselves to the first cause that comes to our mind. If your car isn't running properly, then we won't default to changing the oil. We still need to analyze the different possibilities and look for distinctions. What is different about this car issue? Did it start recently, or has it been going on for a while? Has this happened before, and could it be related to a past issue?

Rushing to solve a problem can make you feel like you're playing whack-a-mole. This is why developing a process, even a simple one, can help you avoid wasting time looking for the cause of a problem. The speed at which you solve a problem matters; after all, solving something quickly is worth more than solving it slowly. Speed needs to be balanced with effectiveness to ensure you're not just throwing darts at a board you can't see.

I worked with a team that had fantastic data, but no one was actually using it. After some analysis, I concluded that the team didn't trust the accuracy of the data, and they didn't know how to build reports easily. In this process, I ran through the possible options and verified each step to uncover the root cause of the problem. My analysis included the following possibilities:

1. Technical issues in the data
2. Wrong technology
3. Lack of trust

4. Lack of training
5. Wrong people in the job

Possibility 1 was easily verifiable through some testing. Possibilities 3 and 4 were confirmed through interviews with the key people. Possibilities 2 and 5 were the most complex causes and the ones with the most assumptions. For example, for 5 to be true, the people in front of me would have to be not doing their jobs across most areas, and this would always have to be the case. It was possible but also unlikely.

Possibilities 3 and 4 ended up being the two causes for this problem. I designed training sessions that would get them over the hump and comfortable working with data. That project was a success, and it was completed in a few weeks. We didn't have to embark on complex technology such as choosing projects or hiring new people. We found the shortest path from A to B.

I love Occam's Razor, but there is also a dark side. I have often seen it in startup culture where "failure" is not just embraced but sought after. It's not about success but how quickly you can fail. I understand the intention behind what these companies are trying to do. Building a company is hard, and you need to "fail" at the wrong ideas before you find the right one. The problem is that the true goal is to grow and succeed.

All this focus on failure can actually lead to failure work. Alan Weiss defined it as "work that's being done because the original attempt was wrong, unsuccessful, or didn't work." Any time something is done twice, you're in the world of failure work. Rushing to solve a problem can put you into failure work, especially if the solution you implement is costly but ineffective at tackling the root cause.

The startups who obsess over failure can also end up in the world of failure work. Rushing through things may cause product launches to fail, money to be spent on the wrong campaigns, and sales deals to be lost because the wrong things were said on a call. Some of this is unavoidable, but a lot of it is not. Think about what would happen if a basketball team took this approach. They would lose the game, but feel great because they took more shots than their opponent. You don't want the fear of failure to hold you back, but you still want to succeed.

Going back to our problem solving, we can prevent this by relying on a process. A good process will consider all the viable options, weigh risks, and think through potential outcomes, good and bad. After going through this process, you can then look for the idea with fewest assumptions, the idea that fits Occam's Razor. You might still not get it right, but you'll get a feel for how to do this quickly and effectively over time.

We spoke about central banks earlier, and I think they get well-deserved credit for how they handled the COVID-19 pandemic. They realized that they needed to inject money into the economy and that giving it to individuals was the fastest way to boost recovery. We saw governments all around the world disperse stimulus checks within days and weeks of making this decision. It was unprecedented how much money was given out in such a short amount of time. I think this is a beautiful example of identifying the root cause of the economic crisis and finding the shortest solution.

BEHIND THE DECISION: THE OTTOMAN EMPIRE CONQUERING OF CONSTANTINOPLE

In 1453, Mehmed II did something that none of his predecessors had been able to achieve. He conquered Constantinople, modern-day Istanbul. Constantinople was the last remaining city of the Roman Empire (or Byzantine Empire). The city had lasted for 1,500 years and survived countless attacks.

There are many aspects of this attack that are significant. Conquering Constantinople allowed the Ottomans to invade mainland Europe, gunpowder was used successfully in this attack, and the fall of the Byzantine Empire is considered a key event in the late Middle Ages.*

I wanted to focus on one element of the attack. Keep in mind that this attack lasted for months, and there were many failures and defeats. However, Mehmed II came up with a brilliant idea halfway through the attack. Constantinople had a harbor that had only one entrance which was heavily fortified. If Mehmed II could get his ships into the harbor, they would have a great position to attack via the water and land.

He knew he couldn't go through the heavily fortified entrance. Instead, he decided to chop down trees to form a path, overland, from where the ships were to inside the harbor. The ships were

---

* "1453: The Fall of Constantinople," World History Encyclopedia, accessed February 21, 2021, https://www.worldhistory.org/article/1180/1453-the-fall-of-constantinople/

carried out of the water, put on greased logs, and moved overnight into the harbor. The Romans were shocked and demoralized to see the ships in the harbor.

The scale of this operation was staggering. The Ottoman army worked for months to cut down trees, grease them, and figure out ways of lifting the ships out of the water. The entire operation had to be done in secret to avoid alerting the Roman army. Mehmed II had to keep the operation secret from his commanders to avoid any leaks and spies.

Putting the ships in the harbor was a key event in the attack and helped tilt the advantage toward the Ottomans. They would go on to break through the city defenses after many battles and skirmishes. The Roman Empire waited on reinforcements from the Vatican, which didn't arrive in time.

It is amazing to see how crazy and yet effective this decision was. Mehmed II truly thought outside the box and beyond any constraints. No one told him that ships could only move through the water, and he didn't let that idea stop him.

DEALING WITH PROBLEMS INSTEAD OF RUNNING AWAY FROM THEM

I wanted to spend the last section of this chapter talking about tough problems. These are the kinds of problems that we tend to put aside until a "better time" or until we "gather more information." The best frameworks can help us clarify the ambiguity, but we still need to take bold action.

In the mid-1970s, Chile's economy was on the brink of high inflation and collapse. Pinochet's regime was looking for answers, and they found them in the so-called Chicago Boys. These were Latin American students who had studied economics at the University of Chicago under Milton Friedman and had come back to their home countries to teach modern economic ideas.

The Chicago Boys didn't have much impact in most of Latin America, but they influenced Pinochet to adopt their theories. Fast forward to 2021, and Chile has one of the strongest economies and the world's most friendly business jurisdiction. They consistently perform better than their neighbors, and the causes can be traced by the decisions made in the 1970s.

The Pinochet regime was a dictatorship that murdered political opponents with ease. One of the few things that they did right was to tackle their debt crisis through effective action. Instead of running away from the hard decisions, they embraced them. Chile isn't perfect, and many things could be improved, but we also have to recognize the success of these decisions.

Today, we can see that countries also learned a few lessons from the 2008 financial crisis. In hindsight, we saw that recovery would have been faster if governments had been willing to spend more money. In the COVID-19 crisis, governments weren't shy about injecting money into the economy. Billions of dollars entered through the government buying bonds, unemployment schemes, and business loans. All this spending is leading toward faster recoveries and a rebounded economy.

In your company and life, take stock of those decisions that are lingering. They could be major, such as firing an employee, or small things like mowing the lawn. Decisions that aren't finalized are worse than those that we get wrong. We have to live with the uncertainty of how this decision will turn out and an extra item on our to-do list. It also leads to overwhelm as we have a mental record of all the things we still need to do.

There isn't much theory that can help here. In most of these decisions, we have to adopt the Nike slogan and just do it. Make some time in your calendar to clean the garage, mow the lawn, review legal contracts, or think through strategy. Make sure that you have tangible outcomes that will be done during that time block. Seeing an outcome like a clean lawn will make it more likely that you will tackle this decision again in the future.

CHAPTER SUMMARY

To understand if a problem is worth solving, answer the following questions:

- What is the problem?
- What is the root cause of the problem?
- Do I care about this problem?

- Read *The Art of Problem Solving* by Russell Ackoff and *The New Rational Manager* by Benjamin Tregoe and Charles Kepner for in-depth problem-solving frameworks.
- Look for the shortest path to your goal (Occam's Razor) while avoiding failure work.
- For your toughest problems, tackle them straight. Adopt the Nike slogan and just do it.

4

The Turtleneck Principle for Making Decisions Once and for All

The 2007 presentation of the iPhone was incredible. I still remember where I was when Steve Jobs started talking about a device that would revolutionize the phone, the iPod, and the web. Seeing him use his finger to scroll through menus, make a phone call, and play "A Little Help from My Friends" from *Sgt. Peppers* felt like peeking into the future.

This presentation would be the first of many Apple presentations that I would watch, and I became accustomed to seeing Steve Jobs in his trademark black turtleneck and blue jeans outfit. I never thought much about his outfit because he wasn't on stage selling clothes. Instead, he was selling the future.

Many years later, I realized that Steve Jobs had taken a decision and converted it into a routine. He didn't have to think about what to wear to work. He simply wore the same thing, making it into his personal brand.

This is one prominent example of the Turtleneck Strategy that we can use to deal with our daily overwhelm. Life is full of decisions that aren't sexy or critical, but they need to be made. What should you discuss with your direct reports? When should you prepare for the upcoming board meeting? Who's picking up the kids from school?

Time is time. It doesn't matter if you're spending it at work or in your personal life. This second strategy will help you carve out more time for the things that matter to you. It will even help you become more consistent with the balls that seemingly keep falling out of the air on a regular basis.

Consistency can be a superpower, especially in our personal lives. Take weight loss, a concern that almost everyone will think about during their lives. Biologically speaking, weight gain and loss happens gradually. You won't gain or lose weight based on one single meal or a single day. The

DOI: 10.4324/9781003185383-4

scale might go up or down, but the body has a certain amount of "water weight," which can shift a few pounds in either direction.

The key to a successful weight loss program is consistency over long periods of time, months, or years. However, the industry tends to focus on short-term strategies to lose weight in seven days or four weeks. You could lose weight in such a short time but just as easily gain it in the following seven days. Without long-term consistency, weight loss can seem elusive.

An extreme example of this yo-yo approach is from "The Biggest Loser," the weight-loss show. The premise of the show is working with obese individuals and helping them lose weight. They are put through strenuous workouts and diets and given all the support they might need. The contestants compete to see how they can lose the most weight during the show. We are talking about hundreds of pounds, which most can do. I don't think I have ever seen a group of people work harder than the people in this show.

Despite their best efforts, *The New York Times* reported that most of these contestants actually gained back their weight within a few years of appearing on the show.* The hundreds of pounds came back, and in some cases even more was added. The issue isn't laziness but biology. The people who appeared on this show became obese over many years, and they have effectively changed their metabolism. Their bodies burn calories at lower rates and have been primed to stay at their obese weight levels.

Blitzing through weight loss sheds the pounds, but it doesn't change their metabolism. Changing how their bodies think about calories will take years of consistent effort. If obesity took ten years to manifest, it's not realistic to expect it to go away in three months. Unfortunately, the body doesn't work like that. The point of this story is that consistency over a long time can be more effective than intensity in the short term.

In business, the same idea applies. The best companies are consistently building toward the future and getting better at their core competencies. Marketing succeeds when you can consistently communicate your message to the right audiences. Growth takes place when you consistently increase revenue and profitability. Executives get better as they consistently execute the right decisions. Daily execution can then compound long-term success. The Turtleneck Principle is meant to help choose long-term consistency in the most important areas of your life.

---

* "After 'The Biggest Loser,' Their Bodies Fought to Regain Weight," *The New York Times*, accessed February 26, 2021, https://www.nytimes.com/2016/05/02/health/biggest-loser-weight-loss.html

WHY YOU SHOULD WEAR THE
SAME OUTFIT EVERY DAY

Steve Jobs started wearing his trademark outfit because he fell in love with uniforms when visiting Japan in the early 1980s. He felt that uniforms provided a sense of unity and community, but the rest of the Apple staff didn't accept the idea. Instead of scrapping it, he adopted it for himself.

Steve Jobs' trademark outfit has been "copied" by other executives. Elizabeth Holmes looked almost like a female version of Steve Jobs while Mark Zuckerberg settled for jeans and a t-shirt. I have also seen the minimalist movement take up a similar idea. Wearing the same pants and shirt every day is a hack for people who don't want to worry about shopping or choosing an outfit in the morning.

Figuring out what to wear or what to eat may seem like minor decisions. They may even seem inconsequential, but every decision we make drains our energy. Worst of all, it's easy to use this knowledge to put off making important decisions, such as providing feedback to your team or carving out time with your romantic partner.

Humans tend to procrastinate. The feeling is strong whenever we are forced to confront things we don't really want to do. The activities are different for everybody. For some, cleaning the garage is torture, while other people enjoy it. For you, it might be working out, or perhaps there are certain activities at work that you simply don't enjoy doing. Being able to complete these activities is the fundamental secret behind all self-help.

The behavior is present even in children. The 1972 Stanford marshmallow experiment is well known within the psychology world. Children were offered a marshmallow now, but they would get more than one marshmallow if they waited for a period of time. The experiment was meant to test how much gratification children could put off and how this might correlate with success later on in life.

Like other psychology experiments, replicating these results isn't easy. Further experiments showed that it wasn't merely about willpower, but economic background also played a role. Nonetheless, the second strategy for making decisions is meant to help tackle the decisions that we tend to put off often.

We can't just ignore these decisions. Instead, we need to convert them into routines that we simply execute like machines. We already know when we will work on new marketing campaigns or eat lunch every day. Maybe it's the same thing, or maybe it's a schedule of options that we cycle through. The point is that we made the decision once instead of hundreds of times.

Let's look at a business example. Peter Drucker famously talked about innovation and abandonment. To innovate, businesses needed to abandon the things that no longer served them, such as unprofitable products, outdated customer segments, and beliefs. Going through this process is sometimes put off in companies to handle the day-to-day challenges. However, if this future work isn't done, the future may not arrive.

We could use the Turtleneck Principle to establish routines and schedules for going through innovation and abandonment. Monthly meetings could be set aside purely to talk about opportunities and what things should be abandoned. Quarterly reviews could include similar questions to prompt managers to start thinking about these topics. Instead of hoping to find time, you make the decision once and then simply execute it.

I hear your objection all the way to my office in Vancouver! You don't want to convert your workday into an emotionless slog through tasks. You don't want to eat the same thing every day. You don't want to wear the same outfit every day. I have good news for you. You don't have to do this.

My goal isn't to suck the joy out of your work or convert you into someone who always wears black regardless of the situation. If you like the idea of brainstorming new ideas or enjoy designing work outfits, go ahead. However, you do have decisions in your life that you could automate or that you should automate because you keep procrastinating on them.

The Turtleneck Principle should tackle those decisions. Be honest with yourself. You can also ask for external help from your partners, colleagues, and bosses. Ask them what activities you tend to skip or procrastinate on. These activities can be prime targets for automation and scheduling.

BEHIND THE DECISION: AMAZON AND AWS

In the year 2000, Amazon was on a mission to sell everything. It wasn't the behemoth it is today, but it was clearly on its way there. The ecommerce industry was still taking baby steps, and Amazon thought there was a business opportunity in helping third-party merchants like Target build online shopping sites. They could leverage Amazon's technology and infrastructure.

The idea flopped after launching a convoluted system without a clear future. They didn't know how to take the different pieces on which Amazon.com ran and make them available to other companies. Andy Jassy, the current Amazon CEO, Jeff Bezos, and others decided that while they couldn't salvage the idea, they could at least fix the internal problems.*

They asked all internal teams to decouple their work and provide API access to other internal teams. This meant that every internal team had to build their products to allow other teams to leverage their work. This was a huge directive that forced many teams to change their product roadmaps. Amazon was hoping that this would allow them to build products faster and avoid duplicating work.

The decoupling effort helped, but it didn't quite solve the problem. Andy Jassy talked to different teams and discovered that they were all building their own resources for each product: databases, storage, etc. When a team did this, they couldn't share their work with other teams quickly enough. Teams were stuck doing repetitive work and losing valuable time.

The executives at Amazon realized that they could use a service that would offer these core services to external customers and, at the very least, to internal teams. It would function as an "operating system for the internet." Being able to provide an infrastructure that was easily accessible could save companies hundreds and thousands of hours, and Amazon was in the right position to create this service.

Amazon Web Services, or AWS for short, launched in 2006 with their EC2 service. The EC2 service allowed companies to spin up cloud servers in minutes and scale them down or up as needed. It actually took years before Google and IBM entered the space, giving Amazon a huge head start into space.

Today, AWS offers more than 175 different services, including cloud computing, data warehouses, identity management, email sending, and much more. The AWS unit generated more than $35 billion dollars in revenue in 2019, and they now power some of the most powerful products globally, including Netflix, Pinterest, and Slack.

---

* "The Myth about How Amazon's Web Service Started Just Won't Die," Networked World, accessed February 28, 2021, https://www.networkworld.com/article/2891297/the-myth-about-how-amazon-s-web-service-started-just-won-t-die.html

The decision to launch AWS proved to be incredibly profitable. The Amazon team didn't know if the idea would work, but it was clearly an issue for them internally, and solving that issue alone would have been worth it. The executive team was also able to explore the question with an open mind and make a consistent process toward launching. It took years before everything came together, but it has proven to be one of the most impactful innovations in the last 20 years.

USING ROUTINES TO TACKLE RECURRING DECISIONS

Humans are habits of routine. Whether or not we consciously designed a routine for our lives, there likely is one. We drive the same routes, go to similar restaurants, and approach our days in a similar fashion. Routines underpin our life, and it's time we take a look at them. Some of them might be perfect, but others could use an upgrade.

Routines can help us minimize the number of things we are thinking about. Think about the most common driving route that you take regularly. The route could be to work or coming home. You likely have an exact series of steps you have adopted over time based on current traffic, time of day, and how you feel. You can go through this route automatically without thinking too much about where you should turn or stop. Imagine if you had to consciously decide every step during your daily driving. You would be exhausted by the time you get to work!

The first step to using routines for decision-making is to take stock of all the things in your life that could be automated. I want you to include all the actions that you do regularly and the actions that you should be doing but somehow don't have time for them. Be sure to include work and personal items. Your list might look like this:

- Presentation for Executive Team
- Meetings with Direct Reports
- Thinking through Strategy
- Prepare Performance Reports
- Analyzing Data and Results
- Providing Feedback to Team

- Eating (Breakfast, Lunch, Dinner)
- Working Out
- Picking Up Children from School
- Date Night
- Playing Golf with Friends

The next step is to prioritize them based on how important they are to you. This is similar to the idea of big and small rocks. We want to tackle the big rocks first before dealing with the small rocks.

For each idea, I then want you to determine the ideal schedule or plan. Don't worry about how you would accomplish this yet because there's plenty of time for that. Start by outlining what you would like to see.

Let's take the idea of meeting with direct reports. You may have a rough outline for what you want to cover during this meeting, but it isn't consistent. These meetings happen at all times, and they sometimes feel pointless. Ideally, you would like to have these meetings in the afternoon so you can spend the morning working on strategic items. You would also like to schedule them on Tuesday and Wednesday, the two days where you aren't as busy.

If you're not sure something could work or if you need the help of someone, ask them. You may need to reshuffle other commitments to make this one work. Also, think about what else you need to make this schedule work. You may need to cancel or reschedule a weekly meeting on Wednesday afternoon or block out these two days for your direct report meetings.

This is how you start to make decisions. You start thinking about the sequence of events that needs to happen instead of just hoping that you'll get through all your direct report meetings.

Now that you have a schedule, make a list of all the things you need to keep this commitment. This could include things like:

- Block off any other meetings between 1 pm and 4 pm in your calendar.
- Get direct reports to book a recurring time going forward.
- Ask each direct report to maintain a document that outlines what they are working on and any questions they have for you.
- Establish a 30-minute block of time on Monday to prepare for the meetings on Tuesday and Wednesday.

You can see that this process can be exhausting. Many details need to be handled, which is why you tend to skip this. You can't work through all these details every week. Instead, things just happen, and meetings end up being booked at random times.

This plan isn't perfect. You might have a board meeting on Tuesday afternoon once a quarter which means you have to reschedule some of your direct report meetings. You might be out of the office on a Monday, so you have to move your prep meeting to Tuesday morning. However, these should be the exception and not the rule. If you still can't stick to a system, you need to analyze what keeps getting in the way and then decide how this should be handled permanently.

The same process applies to the other items on your list based on their priority. If you enjoy a certain decision like choosing where to eat lunch, don't convert it into a routine. Notice what things you enjoy, what things you dread, and what things you're indifferent about.

In my experience, decisions are finalized when they are added to your calendar or when you share them with your team and family. Let them know that you're busy from 6 pm to 7 pm with the gym and can't attend meetings past 4:30 pm. Most people will adjust to your schedule without any difficulties. The hard part is making the decision.

I also want to make a special note of those important decisions that fall through the cracks. Date nights are a perfect example. It's common for both partners to be busy and for date nights to keep being postponed.

You can use this system with your partner to establish a blocked time for date night. It might be once a week or once a month. You then make the necessary adjustments to maintain this commitment. Your health, family, and team will be better off in the long term when these decisions are made.

The most creative people in the world were known for their consistent routines. Gustave Flaubert famously said, "Be regular and orderly in your life, so that you may be violent and original in your work." Churchill would wake up at 7:30 am but remain in bed for several hours reading and eating breakfast. On the other hand, Ben Franklin woke up at 4 am and started work at 8 am. There's no magic formula here, but it is about finding the right routine for you.

I'll also note the question of how early you should start your day. There's a general pressure to start the day as early as possible which could be 3 am or 4 am. I disagree with the general statement but agree that an early start tends to be beneficial. I'm specifically talking about starting your day by 7 am versus 11 am. However, the start of your day should align with your body clock and the culture around you.

We all have a body clock that leans toward being more alert in the morning or at night, making us night owls versus early risers. I'm personally more of a night owl, but I still aim to start my day by 7 am. If I'm not careful, I can easily stay up to 3 am or 4 am, pushing my wake-up time to 10 am or 11 am. Some people naturally wake up by 6 am and fall asleep by 10 pm. Find your internal clock and experiment if needed.

There's also a question about the culture around you. Argentinians and Spaniards tend to eat dinner late, 9 pm or later. If you plan to sleep early, you might end up missing a significant portion of the social life that takes place in the city. There's no right or wrong here, but aligning yourself to the clock of your city tends to be helpful. The same goes for countries where afternoon naps are commonplace.

Finally, make sure that you're getting enough rest. Our culture values the person who can sleep little and work long hours, but our decision-making ability suffers from poor sleep. You'll hear people say that you should make your most important decisions in the morning when you're freshest. I think part of this comes down to people spending too little time sleeping, so they are only alert during the morning and start to fade in the afternoon.

I think you should aim to be alert for most of the day, and you accomplish that by sleeping more. Parents with newborn children are exempt from this, as their sleep schedule is out of their control, but if you don't have young kids, then tweak your schedule to allow for more sleep. If you don't believe me, try it for yourself. Spend two weeks sleeping at least seven to eight hours and notice how you feel and perform at work. The chances are high that things will seem or be easier simply because you have more mental energy.

DOES YOUR TEAM KNOW WHAT TO DO REGULARLY?

Routines aren't just helpful in your personal life. They can even help your team accomplish more at work. Every team has a series of tasks that need to be done regularly. Some teams do this in a relaxed fashion, while other teams struggle to get everything done on time. Like in our personal examples, consistent issues are reflections of poor systems.

Your team already has routines. Meetings are a great example of routines that almost every team does today. We want to take the concept of routines beyond just meetings and help everyone on your team get organized around the important things.

To go through this process, schedule a meeting with relevant team members to run them through the same process we ran in the previous section. You can spend some time explaining why this matters and how you're using it in your life. The goal is to become proactive about important elements of their work. For example, you may notice that your team struggles to go through customer complaints. Assign someone to own this task who can spend one hour on Monday afternoon going through the latest responses and sharing them in a weekly team meeting.

The great thing about doing this in teams is that it gives everyone a chance to determine how they want to engage with the company. Some people prefer to work uninterrupted in the mornings, while others want to spend the afternoons without any distractions. Getting everyone to prioritize the actions they need to do and then work on scheduling them will show you why conflicts are always happening.

Once everyone completes the process, gather them back together in a second meeting to look at their goals and schedules. You can now work on establishing the activities that need teamwork, including meetings and projects. Some team members might compromise on their original vision, but everyone should feel more in control of their schedule and decisions.

One of my favorite work activities is helping teams optimize their time. Teams put up with "necessary evils," but these evils can take up all your time over time. I worked with a client who was seeing a drop in sales performance. They were frantically trying to solve it through endless meetings. It seemed like nothing was progressing except the total amount of meeting time.

I worked with them to take a step back and run through a problem-solving exercise. They then decided on the best possible solutions, gave themselves enough time to try them out, and scheduled a follow-up meeting to review and adjust their course. As you might imagine, they started making progress in restoring the sales performance standards.

Executives and teams need to consistently analyze how they spend their time and energy. I believe that long workdays exist because of unclear time management. Why should your weekly review meeting be 60 minutes? Why can't it be done in 30 minutes? Do you have to meet with your counterpart every week, or could it be done twice a week? I always tell executives that they should try changing the frequency and length of their most time-consuming engagements. If it doesn't work, you can always revert.

In the COVID-19 pandemic, most companies were forced to become remote-friendly. Overnight, video conferences were set up, VPN access was provided, and computer equipment was upgraded. As it turns out, companies can work remotely. In some cases, the remote aspect was much better than the in-person equivalent. After the pandemic, I expect many companies to go back into the office while maintaining a hybrid approach to their teams. Trying different ways of working isn't fatal, and in most cases, you will learn something new.

BEHIND THE DECISION: BREXIT

In June 2016, the world looked with anticipation toward the UK to see if they would choose to leave the European Union. David Cameron's government had decided to run a country-wide referendum to ask the citizens whether they should stay or depart the international coalition of governments. As a surprise result, 52% voted to leave, splitting the country on a major political decision.

The withdrawal was originally set for March 2019, but it didn't actually occur until January 31, 2020. The UK left the EU after being a member for 47 years. The UK wasn't one of the "founding" countries and, in fact, had trouble joining the original coalition after their application was a veto by Charles de Gaulle, the French president, in 1963 and 1967.

The desire to leave the union wasn't new in Britain. They never fully embraced the union, choosing to keep their currency, the British pound, instead of adopting the euro. In the 1970s and 1980s, the Labour Party in Britain ran on a campaign to leave the EU, and a referendum was run in 1975. At that time, 62.2% of the electorate voted to stay in. The skepticism toward the EU continued to grow for the next 40 years.

The results of 2016 followed a global trend in a split of political opinions. People in smaller towns voted to leave in higher numbers compared with people in bigger cities. Older people also voted to leave compared to younger voters. Britain saw a common split between small and big cities and between conservatives and liberals.

Older voters are more likely to vote than younger voters, which led to a slight advantage for leaving.

The impact of Brexit isn't fully understood yet. The withdrawal process was messy and complicated. Multiple Prime Ministers lost their jobs, and Britain had to consistently get extensions to figure out the contract negotiation. Britain can't simply just leave, as the EU is one of their biggest trading partners. The EU, on the other hand, needs to maintain an advantage for their members under which Britain no longer qualifies.

The decision to leave has been in the making since Britain joined the EU. Support for the single economic system doesn't seem to have ever taken hold in Britain. However, after 47 years of living under this model, the breakup will be messy. Companies will be forced to change headquarters to keep operating under the EU system, British nationals will likely experience issues traveling into the EU, and a host of factors will come up in the next few years.

It is widely expected that leaving the EU will have negative short-term effects on Britain. However, the future is unclear. Britain could take on a bigger role on the global stage, free from EU politics. Britain could also improve their relationships with partners like the United States and Canada. The possibilities are endless, but they will depend on what kind of political strategy is adopted. Shrinking in their role isn't likely to benefit Britain now that they are swimming alone in a global sea.

OPTIMIZING YOUR ROUTINES AND SYSTEMS

Making decisions once will be one of the most beneficial actions you can take. However, you should also be ready to change them as circumstances change. For example, I love to spend the summers in Vancouver exploring nature through hikes and biking. I typically shorten my workday to still have time for the gym and an outdoor bike ride before the sunsets. In the winter, I swapped the bike ride for walks.

Humans are incredibly adept at dealing with change. We constantly change every day as we deal with traffic, unexpected problems, and unforeseen events. Your routines and automated decisions should be able to bend to adjust to circumstances. A work crisis pop up that is threatening your gym time? Move the gym back an hour or schedule it for tomorrow. If the same event keeps coming up often, you may need to relook at the cause of the event itself.

All our lives have a seasonal cadence driven by the weather, our partners, our kids, and our work. The decisions and schedules we create aren't going to change much every week, but they should change a few times a year to reflect these seasonal flows. With that being said, here are a few guidelines for how to optimize your routines and systems:

- Make a note of activities that keep falling through the cracks. You may still need more support or changes to deal with other parts of your schedule.
- Think about how to decrease the time needed for any given action. Don't assume that preparing for a board meeting will always take you 90 minutes. You may be able to shorten that to 60 minutes.
- It's okay to change things once they stop working. Perhaps you have a favorite breakfast that you loved for six months, but you now dread it. Decide to change it and try something new.
- Become good at saying no and protecting your schedule. Most people are open to multiple options, and the one they pick doesn't have to conflict with your preferred choice.
- Simplify how you track and remember these decisions. It isn't about adding new technology but about reducing the friction to track and complete tasks.

Routines will be a guiding lighthouse during your busiest days. You'll be able to go on autopilot because you trust your schedule and your decisions. You will still get through the items you care about the most, despite what life throws at you.

CHAPTER SUMMARY

- Converting decisions into routines and systems isn't just about saving time but also ensuring that you find the time to work on strategy while supporting your direct reports.

- Routines won't suck the joy out of your life. Instead, they allow you to spend time doing the things you truly love.
- Block out time to design how you want to spend your days and weeks and what needs to happen to prevent conflicts.
- Work with your team to proactively tackle their week instead of responding to incoming requests.
- Be open to optimizing and changing your routines based on seasonal changes and other factors.

5

Using the 3 Os Framework
for the Critical Few

Have you ever solved a Sudoku puzzle? These puzzles have nine grids, each with three rows and three columns. Inside each grid, you have to write the numbers 1 through 9 in the correct boxes. The nine numbers should not repeat within the grid, and they should not repeat across the vertical and horizontal lines of the entire puzzle.

Sudoku is a math exercise in running through different possibilities and seeing what fits. You may think that the best answer in this box is a 4 until you realize that another box is better suited for that 4. I'm not particularly good at Sudoku, but I think it serves as a great analogy for this chapter.

Imagine trying to solve a Sudoku without knowing the rules. You don't know about the no repeating rule of how each grid works with the others. You simply try to fill numbers based on random logic. You would never solve the puzzle, and it would be an incredibly frustrating experience. The same can happen when we make major decisions. Without a process or a set of rules, going through major decisions can feel like walking a tightrope with no net to catch us.

We previously talked about two strategies for dealing with decisions: problem-solving and the Turtleneck principle. The first strategy was meant to help us clarify exactly what problem we are solving and avoid spinning our wheels on the wrong problems. The second strategy was meant to help us automate decisions that are important but tend to be repetitive. These two strategies are trying to reduce the mental burden of decisions and preserve our energy.

In the third strategy, we get to use all the energy we have preserved. By this point, we are dealing with the most important decisions in our lives.

DOI: 10.4324/9781003185383-5

It could involve deciding on what new market to enter, what person to hire to lead our new unit on innovation, or working with our children to determine what colleges they should apply for. There's no avoiding these decisions, and we need a process that can increase the chances that we make the right decisions. Without a process, every decision will feel precarious and full of danger.

I will introduce the 3 Os framework, a three-step process for making decisions. There are many decision frameworks out there, some going all the way to ten steps. I'm not sure if anyone can even remember ten steps, which is why I wanted to keep my framework simple. It has been inspired by the framework design by Ben Tregoe and Charles Kepner. I'll show you the similarities later on in this chapter and why I decided to make certain changes.

THE REMAINING CRITICAL FEW

Getting certain decisions right is critical. Think about situations when executives or teams made the wrong decision. It's not from malice but from failing to see potential obstacles or risks. I was reading recently about Bill Michael, the managing chairman of KPMG in the UK. He resigned from his job after telling his employees to "stop moaning about the pandemic"* in a virtual meeting. He was trying to communicate that employees shouldn't complain about their situations, including endless Zoom meetings, working from home, and dealing with restrictions.

The call eventually leaked, and he was forced to resign. Bill Michael didn't foresee all the consequences from his remarks. It turns out that he was ignoring public health regulations and was likely fed up with the pandemic. However, everyone is fed up with the pandemic, and every situation is different. I'm sure that KPMG employees are happy that they get to keep their jobs and work from home, but it doesn't make it easier for them. These kinds of decisions happen all the time, and having a better framework can help minimize the impact of bad decisions.

---

* KPMG's Bill Michael Resigns after Telling Staff to 'Stop Moaning,'" *The Guardian*, accessed March 1, 2021, https://www.theguardian.com/business/2021/feb/12/kpmg-bill-michael-resigns-after-telling-staff-to-stop-moaning

In your life and work, you likely have a good sense of the critical few decisions that will make a significant impact. We commonly hear about choosing the right partner, choosing where to live, and choosing the right team as some of the most important decisions. Yet, we don't always give these decisions the proper care that they require. We may spend more time deciding where to go on vacation than who we will spend most of our free time with.

There is something paradoxical about these critical decisions. On the one hand, we need to give them the appropriate amount of thinking and deliberation. On the other hand, speed matters. Making high-quality decisions rapidly is better than making high-quality decisions slowly. However, we don't want to let the speed deteriorate the quality of our decisions. The solution is to have a framework that is nimble, memorable, and easily applicable. The 3 Os is the ideal framework for this.

I'm fascinated by how major decisions are made. I spoke previously about the poor critical thinking that took place during the pandemic. I have also been following Britain's strategy. I covered Brexit in a previous chapter, and we now get to see how Britain will approach being a standalone country. One of the decisions that is being debated as I write this is how to think about innovation. Every country wants to modernize its economy and ensure that it can keep up in our global world.

Britain has decided to create an organization similar to DARPA, which played a huge role in driving innovation within the United States. DARPA had a hand in creating the internet, computer networking, and even the graphical interfaces in computers. Britain's plan lacks detail, but they are heading in the right direction. Britain realizes that the best defense is a good offense, and they need to take a leadership role in the world. After leaving the EU, Britain can't "hide" among European countries anymore. I think that Britain has the right conditions for an influential global country, but I'm not sure if the politics align with this vision.

In our personal lives, critical decisions are perhaps even more important. They involve decisions around how much time we spend with our family, how we educate our children, and how we treat ourselves. Lack of time is one of the biggest challenges for executives, which leads to something falling through the cracks. Family time tends to be one of the loose pieces to trickle through. I work with executives to help them understand how to better spend their energy on the most impactful areas. We primarily look at what decisions are being made and how to enable their teams to get better at making the right decisions even under pressure.

Children's education is another critical area that can benefit from the 3 Os framework. Most of my clients have the ability to pay for private schooling, but they still need to determine what role they will play in their children's education. What school should you send them to? What values do you want to impart? How do you want to spend your summers? What happens when the school system falls short of your expectations?

Imagine being a parent in COVID-19. We are seeing battles take place between school boards and parents. Teachers are unwilling to go back to classrooms until they feel safer, and parents are frustrated at the lack of education, even if it takes place online. Data shows that missing school is incredibly harmful to children's overall development, affecting poorer families more. Teachers also have a valid point about safety and what it means for them and their families. These aren't easy decisions, and they are fraught with obstacles, politics, and emotions.

I can't promise a framework that will solve all of your challenges and questions. Situations like the one I mentioned with the school board are incredibly complex. We can't control what others do, but we can control our decisions. The goal is to understand what factors are under our control and how we think through all the options and obstacles associated with any given decision. I think this is the kind of training that should be taught in schools. We should be teaching our children to think critically and how to analyze situations on their own. That's a skill that you can use for the rest of your life.

BEHIND THE DECISION: MARVEL SELLING ITS SUPERHEROES AND THEIR REDEMPTION

In 1997, Marvel Enterprises filed for bankruptcy. Ten years after its incorporation, the public company had run out of money. It was operating in a shrinking market after comic books lost their value in the 90s. During this time, Marvel decided to sell the rights to some of their most popular characters: Spider-Man, the X-men, and others.[*]

In 2005, Marvel was renamed Marvel Entertainment to reflect their focus on financing movies based on their characters. They were

[*] "How Marvel Went from Bankruptcy to Billions," Den of Geek, accessed March 2, 2021, https://www.denofgeek.com/movies/how-marvel-went-from-bankruptcy-to-billions/

encouraged by the success of Sony and Fox, which had released successful films. Marvel made very little profit from these partnerships and thought they could do a better job on their own. Kevin Feige imagined a shared universe where all the characters could coexist. He was soon appointed as the studio chief at just 33 years old.

Fast forward to today, and Marvel is a powerhouse in movies. The Walt Disney Company acquired Marvel Entertainment for $4 billion, and the Marvel movies have done incredibly well. As of November 2020, the Marvel Cinematic Universe series was the highest-grossing film franchise in the world, with a total worldwide box office revenue of $22.56 billion. Each film generated an average of $980.5 million.

Quite a drastic change for a company that was bankrupt merely ten years before launching their film division. The Marvel movies are so impactful that they tend to dominate box offices whenever they are released. Marvel is now adding TV shows and other media to complement their ever-expanding universe. The moves also tend to do generally well with critics, and fans love them.

There are several decisions that Marvel took along this journey. First, there was the decision to sell their most important characters. It took Marvel some time and negotiating to bring back Spider-Man and the X-men. They couldn't reference them in their movies for years, and they had to watch Sony, Fox, and others miss the mark in their movies. The external partners made profitable films that fans hated.

Nonetheless, Marvel made those decisions based on the context of the 1990s. Comic books weren't that popular, no one had made a good comic book movie, and they needed the money. Ten years later, as conditions changed, Marvel realized that they could produce movies on their own and likely do it better than their external partners. They approached them just like the comics and gave individual directors the freedom to be creative while aligning with the overall creative goals.

The decision to make their own movies was bold, but I think Marvel realized that they had several advantages going for them. They also noticed the growing trend of films and the success of other comic book movies like *The Dark Knight* series from Warner Brothers. Their execution was excellent, and teaming up with Disney paired them up with another studio that consistently understands how to deliver great films.

Don't assume that all of this would have happened without the right decisions. We have the counterexample in Warner Brothers who also decided to create their own cinematic universe called the DC Extended Universe (DCEU). The movies have done decently well in revenue, bringing in around $5 billion. The movies have not done as well critically, and they have often felt disjointed. The studio has also been unable to keep continuity with several key characters like Batman being recast.

Warner Brothers has the playbook from Marvel but hasn't been able to execute the process as well as Marvel did. The decisions companies make shape them for years, and this is why learning to make better decisions is a crucial skill. I don't think either company has more talent than the other. A different culture simply surrounds them, and that might just make all the difference.

THE 3 OS FRAMEWORK: USING RINGS TO HIT THE GOAL

For critical decisions, we can use a framework or process. This might feel like an overly complex or rigorous approach, but as you will see below, all of us already have some kind of process in which we make decisions. The challenge is that we aren't aware of our process, making it difficult to improve or teach. Teaching is important, especially if you're leading a team that would like to emulate you.

Let's start by trying to understand how we currently make decisions. This will be hard mental work but stick with me. Think back to the last two to three major decisions that you made in the last few months. Skip all the minor ones like where to go for lunch or what color you should paint your house. You have those two to three decisions in your mind? Let's go through some questions.

- What was the first thing that you thought about? Solutions? Options? What do you want to accomplish? Why do you even have to make this decision?
- How did you process all the variables? Did you write them down? Mentally keep track of them? Talk with a friend or colleague?

- Did you keep coming back to specific parts of the decision e.g. risk, downside, etc.?
- How long did it take you to make the decision? This could be minutes, hours, days, weeks, or even longer.
- Was it an enjoyable experience, or are you dreading the next time you will have to go through this again?

Now that you have thought about your current process, write it down on paper in a logical sequence. Imagine that you have a major decision to make this week and you want to take it through your decision-making process. On paper, write down the first thing you would do, the second, the third, and so on. Be as detailed as you want and include any external help such as talking to a friend or to your partner. Estimate how long the process should take based on previous experiences.

You will have in front of you how you currently make decisions. This simple exercise is huge because it is starting to expose one of the most important mental processes. On paper, you could now make adjustments, add steps or perhaps even remove them altogether. You would also be able to teach it to other people. Finally, you can compare it against other frameworks to see how yours stacks up, which we will do.

Sia is one of our generation's most prolific songwriters behind hits like "Chandelier" and "Cheap Thrills." She has also written for some of the best artists including Rihanna, Britney Spears, and Katy Perry. The surprising part is that her songwriting process is quite simple. She receives a track (the beat), she will then add a melody of gibberish and then replace that with actual words.

Sia has done this in under 15 minutes for some of her biggest hits.[*] The key is that she has a process in which she can improve and optimize over time. Making a hit isn't something that happens through random conditions for her. She represents the side of artists where creating music can be formulaic and consistent instead of waiting for inspiration to hit. In decisions, we can also replicate this idea by consistently running through the correct process.

Let's now talk about the 3 Os framework. The framework has three major components: Outcomes, Options and Obstacles. I'll explain each

---

[*] "Sia: 'I Wrote "Chandelier" in about 15 Minutes,'" Press Party, accessed March 4, 2021, https://www. pressparty.com/pg/newsdesk/Sia/view/112048/

component below, but they are structured logically so you would first determine the ideal outcomes, weigh all the options to get you there, and think about potential obstacles that could get in your way. As you go through each component or step, you are narrowing down options until you get to the best decision for this specific situation. Best in this case means that it aligns with your goals and could be achievable by your team or yourself. There are few guarantees in life, except for death and taxes, but we are trying to increase the probability of success here (Figure 5.1).

As you can see in the image above, the metaphor for this framework is a a series of rings. The first ring refers to Outcomes, the second ring is Options, and the third ring is Obstacles. After you have gone through the framework, you will end up at the center or ideal decision. The metaphor also helps us understand the narrowing process. As you go through each ring, you will be filtering potential options. You have fewer options and items to consider in the second ring than in the first one. Once we decide on an outcome, we are limited in the options that could get us that outcome, and once we choose the appropriate option, the list of obstacles is even smaller.

My framework is inspired by Ben Tregoe and many others who have similar three level frameworks. I'm not a fan of frameworks that have eight or nine steps, as I think that is too much to remember. On the other hand, three is an easy number to remember, and organizing them under the same letter (O) makes it even easier. Remember that my goal here is to give you a framework that you can eventually internalize and make your own. You should be able to make decisions naturally and rapidly. If you need to

3 Os Framework

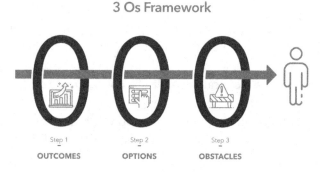

FIGURE 5.1
3 Os framework.

write on easels or a whiteboard to make a decision, you will be limited by how often you can use it.

The first component of the framework is Outcomes. We start here because it doesn't matter how hard we work or how smart we are if we end up at the wrong destination. You could be running very fast, but you won't get anywhere if you're on a treadmill. The same applies for outcomes. Spending significant resources, time, and money, to end up at the wrong outcome is wasteful. One of the major issues that happens when we make decisions is that we wrongly assumed the outcome that we want. If you have ever driven in the wrong directions for more than a few minutes, then you know how frustrating this can be. Imagine "driving in the wrong direction" with an entire team or company, and you can see why this would be the first step.

I love working out, and over time, I have explored other sports like bouldering. This is when you do rock climbing without ropes. Typically, you're going up artificial rocks or you're doing it outside. Either way, you're only climbing a few feet up in the air unless you're fearless and you're willing to go up a mountain without any safety. If you have ever seen the documentary *Free Solo* by Alex Honnold, then you know how crazy this can be. Nonetheless, becoming strong at the gym is different from becoming strong at bouldering. You need to train appropriately for the right sport. Depending on what outcome I want, I will need to figure out the ideal options. I could spend weeks or months training on the wrong things!

When thinking of outcomes, you want to spend time thinking of how things could be. This exercise is easier for some people than others, but it is crucial for everyone. Try to move away from what is happening today and think of the ideal scenario in the future. I understand that this can be hard, as current events will shape our imagination of the future. If you're stuck dealing with customer problems in the present, you might find it hard to imagine a world where that isn't the case. This is the time to suspend judgment and dream freely. Run through the following questions.

- What do I wish would happen in this situation or decision?
- If I had a 100% guarantee of an outcome, what would that be?
- If I/we (we as in team), could do anything without fear or hesitation, what would we do?
- If I achieve this outcome, will I be satisfied or happy?

- What are the unexpected consequences of achieving this outcome?
- Are there other outcomes that could get me what I want?

The questions are meant to help you evaluate all the different outcomes that could make sense in this situation. If you're thinking of growth for your company, you also need to think about profit and how growth could backfire. You may realize that you don't want to grow your company at all costs; instead, you want more free time with your family. Or you may realize that what you really care about is profitability, and that's what you should focus on. Or growth may be your true outcome, and now you feel more strongly about it once you thought through different possibilities.

We tend to stick to an answer or goal once we attach enough emotional energy to it. Being able to suspend some of this emotion can help us explore the wide range of possibilities. Imagine someone who undertakes a career like law or medicine just to realize that they find the law boring or can't stand to see blood. We won't always capture these realizations, but we can at least make an effort to think through them. It's also helpful to imagine what would happen if we achieved this outcome. Are you going to spend more time working? Are you going to feel healthier? Are you going to still need to work on another goal? Assume that you have achieved an outcome, does life look as expected to you?

I'm fascinated by how NASCAR is trying to deal with racism.[*] Their fan base skews white and of all the drivers, only one of them is black as of early 2021. Only around 8% and 9% NASCAR fans are black and Latino respectively. Obviously, this could be an issue for NASCAR long term. Sports want to grow, and you do that by appealing to the groups of people who don't currently watch your sports. At the same time, NASCAR needs to deal with these issues without alienating their current fans. The viewership of NASCAR has been declining since 2014, and this might be accelerated as they became part of the larger political conversion in 2020.

NASCAR needs to think about what outcome they truly want for their sport. Focusing just on the perception of racism might not be enough to attract new fans, and they might lose fans in the aggregate. I think NASCAR should think of ways to make the sport more interesting for

---

[*] "Nascar Failed to Fight Racism for 72 Years. Don't Praise Its Support of Bubba Wallace Yet," *The Guardian*, accessed March 8, 2021, https://www.theguardian.com/sport/2020/jun/23/nascar-bubba-wallace-racism-talladega-wendell-scott

non-fans, either by adding more excitement or changing the rules of racing. They should also make a deliberate effort to bring drivers of other races into the sport. I would be looking toward the British F1 league where Lewis Hamilton dominates the sport. F1 is also dealing with their own issues of racism, but their sport has managed to maintain relevance in our rapidly changing world.

As you think through your ideal outcomes, it can be helpful to talk to other people to bounce ideas. This will naturally happen within companies, but think about it for your personal life. Sometimes we can't even see a possibility until someone else has done it. If you're thinking of an outcome for an area like fitness, consider talking to a coach who can help you understand the range of outcomes you could be exploring. Whenever I get pushback on this idea, I'm surprised, as a few hundred dollars could completely change your perspective on what is possible. It's easier than ever to talk to an expert on nearly every topic in the world.

As you go through this process, you may find it easier to write your ideas down. I talked about not wanting to rely on easels or paper, but as you learn the process, these devices can help. You eventually want to be able to run through this framework in your head, but there's always going to be situations where there are too many variables to think about. The power of journaling has been somewhat lost in our culture, but it can be a fantastic way to see connections that aren't clearly seen mentally. You can also run through each potential outcome, take notes and then physically cross it out as you analyze it.

The second step in the framework is options. Once you determine the ideal outcome for this decision, you can explore the different ways of getting there. There's almost always multiple ways of getting to the same outcome. This is important because we can get stuck thinking that we only have the option or only one thing could be done in this situation. This kind of binary thinking (either I do it or I don't) is a clear sign that we haven't fully explored this decision and everything it entails. Emotions may be running high, and we might be blinded—literally—from seeing all the different options in front of us.

I'll admit that we may not enjoy the options that are in front of us. Tough decisions involve compromise, but there are multiple ways of accomplishing the same goal. If you find that you can't think of more than one option, you may need to go back to the first step and redefine your outcome. If your outcome is to get your daughter into a good college, there are multiple options. If your outcome is to get your daughter into Stanford Medicine in September of this year, your options will be limited. I would still expect to see multiple options to get there to Stanford but the tighter your outcome, the fewer the options.

I also want to make a note about decisions that affect others. I have seen a pattern where we impose our preferences into decisions that don't actually affect us. I was talking to a friend who wanted to travel once the COVID-19 pandemic was over. He was unsure of taking the vaccine despite the growing evidence of its safety. Putting aside my preferences or opinions, I can see that he could still accomplish his goal of traveling internationally without a vaccine. He could get negative COVID-19 tests, he could look for places that don't require a vaccine, or he could simply wait until the situation changes.

Imposing my preferences would mean that his only option for traveling abroad is to get the vaccine, but that's not the case. This separation is harder to do when we deal with family and our work team. We may have a sense of the "right" option, but we need to walk a fine line between ordering someone to do something and simply providing advice. Getting someone to buy into an option can be more powerful than simply forcing them to take it. Being able to accept options that we wouldn't choose is also an important part of this process.

Once you have multiple options, you can rank them. One option will be a better fit for your situation, and we want an objective way of processing all the data that we have. I recommend that you make a list of the criteria that each option needs to satisfy and divide them into two categories: critical and optional. The option's critical items must be met, and optional items aren't required as stated by their name. Here are some questions to explore as you define your criteria.

- What must happen for each option to be successful?
- What would be nice to have in each option?
- How can I verify that something is critical or optional?
- If I achieved an option but still failed to hit my outcome, what was missing?

Let's imagine that your outcome is to reduce the acquisition cost of a new customer. Your options are as follows: assigning an internal person to audit your marketing campaigns or bringing an external expert to run the audit. The criteria for these options will be broken down into critical and optional.

Critical Criteria

Deep expertise in digital channels such as Facebook and Google
Experience with million-dollar advertising budgets
Understanding of your industry and benchmarks

Optional Criteria

Past experience running similar audits
Experience with offline channels
Located within the San Francisco area
Fits within certain budget expectations (Table 5.1)

We can now assign weight to each criterion. The critical items should get a weight of ten while the optional should get a weight of five. We may have an option that does well on the optional criteria but does poorly on the critical. We wouldn't want that to take over our calculation and give preference to an option that may not be the best fit. Based on those scores, we can see that the total score on the critical section is 30 (10 × 3), the optional section is 20 (5 × 4), and the total score is 50 (30 + 20).

We can also discard any options that fail to meet the critical criteria. If we meet an external partner that doesn't have experience with million

TABLE 5.1

Ranking Options against Criteria

Criteria	Weight	Score
Deep expertise in digital channels such as Facebook and Google (Critical)	10	8
Experience with million-dollar advertising budgets (Critical)	10	7
Understanding of your industry and benchmarks (Critical)	10	9
Past experience running similar audits (Optional)	5	5
Experience with offline channels (Optional)	5	4
Located within the San Francisco area (Optional)	5	5
Fits within certain budget expectations (Optional)	5	5
Fit Score	50	43

dollar budgets, we can exclude them altogether. The Critical criteria are things that we cannot compromise on and must be met by every single option that we are exploring. We may have options that rank poorly on these items, but they at least meet them in some shape or form.

We can now rank each option on each item to the best of our abilities. At this stage, you would run through whatever research is needed to better understand each option. You may also end up with multiple sub-options. For example, the marketing options listed above might include multiple external partners who would each get ranked under our criteria. At the end, we want to have a total score for each item, what I would call a "fit score". If an option scored 36 out of 50, we can say that the fit score for this option is 72% (36/50).

You'll notice that very few options will score a perfect 100% score. That's to be expected, as things rarely match all of our expectations. We are looking for the best fit based on the critical and optional criteria. You may also realize that items need to be shuffled around. Some things need to become critical, and perhaps you need to convert others into optional. This shuffling is common, especially if you're dealing with a decision you haven't faced before and don't know what is appropriate or normal.

Trying to compare options without a set of objective criteria leads to chaos. You may end up with the most emotionally charged option, or you might choose the option that is easiest. Think of car dealerships and how they are adapting to electric cars. Should they have shown electric cars alongside gas cars? Electric car buyers may be turned off by this, especially since we are still in the early adopter stage. They might be better off creating entirely new dealerships just for electric cars and treating them as drastically different customer segments. Being able to weigh their options and run through criteria can make these kinds of decisions straightforward.

The third and final component is obstacles. Now that we know our ideal outcome and the best option to get there, we need to think about what could get in our way. I learned how to code when I was 15, and I adopted an engineering mindset. I tended to default to solutions once I heard a problem. The problem with jumping to solutions too quickly is that we may miss obstacles that can completely derail us. If you have ever made a decision that didn't turn out as expected, obstacles may be the culprit. The solution is to try your hardest to find the holes in your best fit option.

We'll do this by looking for anything that could prevent us from achieving our outcome. The obstacles can include things within our control, such as hiring the wrong person or things outside of our control such as the economy going into recession. Either way, we can think about how to mitigate and eliminate these obstacles. The classic phrase of "an ounce of prevention is worth a pound of cure" is the motto of the third step.

My favorite framework for thinking through obstacles comes from Alan Weiss.* He talked about preventive and contingent actions. Preventive actions are taken to prevent a problem from occurring, while contingent actions are taken to minimize the damage caused by a problem. Let's use the example of fires. Preventative actions include establishing fire building codes and fire alarms. Contingent actions include fire extinguishers, firefighters, and water sprinklers.

Preventive actions main goal is to prevent the fire from ever taking place. They are the most effective way to spend resources. If a fire takes place, sprinklers and firefighters are there to contain the fire. The problem is that even if sprinklers work perfectly, the fire will still cause some damage. We shouldn't rely on contingent actions, but we still need them. In our framework, we can think of obstacles through these two dimensions to better understand the unexpected risks. Think through the following questions.

- What could go wrong with the option I chose in step 2?
- How could I prevent and deal with (contingent) any obstacles?
- If everything went wrong with my ideal option, what would I need to do to get back on track?
- What are the steps that I would need to take to solve an obstacle?
- Are there any obstacles that would cause my option to completely fail?

You will still come across obstacles that you didn't think about, that's normal. These kinds of obstacles fall into the "unknown unknowns" category that Donald Rumsfeld, ex-Secretary of Defense, talked about. Don't get caught up in the things that you can't think about. Focus on the obvious obstacles that come up right away and work on mitigating

---

* "Preventive vs Contingent," Alan Weiss, accessed March 16, 2021, https://alanweiss.com/preventi ve-vs-contingent/

them. Even spending a few minutes thinking through obstacles will start to change how you make decisions. Our plan of attack may be perfect, but if we don't expect the enemy to adapt, we are going into battle unprepared.

Thinking through obstacles ahead of time may be a superpower. On January 6, 2021, protestors gathered outside Capitol Hill in the United States. They were protesting against the claims of voting fraud in the 2020 presidential election between Trump and Biden. Eventually, the protestors broke through the barriers and they stormed the Capitol building where officials were certifying the election results. Everyone was evacuated and it took hours before protestors were peacefully removed from the building.

Seeing pictures of protestors sitting in the chair of the Speaker of the House was chilling. However, do you think that this scenario was not on the radar of people who were planning the security for this protest? I highly doubt that no one said "what if protestors overwhelm security, and they storm the building?" If you consider this a potential obstacle, you could then determine the appropriate preventive and contingent measures. Perhaps security numbers were too low, or perhaps protestors were too close to the building itself. Whatever it was, a lack of obstacle planning was one of the guilty parties. Lessons were learned for Biden's inauguration, which took place a few weeks later.

That covers the explanation of the 3 Os framework. Spend some thinking through each step and how you did it in your day to day decisions. In the next few sections, I want to show you how to internalize the framework and eventually throw it away. My goal is for this kind of thinking to become a background process in your mind that you can fall back on even in your most difficult moments.

LEARNING THE FRAMEWORK AND THROWING IT AWAY

Knowing how to learn is one of the most underrated skills in our world today. It's one thing to memorize facts, but it's another to understand the relationship between them and the best way for us to get to this understanding. I didn't learn this lesson while in school, and I actually did quite poorly in university. High school was easier because you could just memorize your way to high marks, but university requires a deeper understanding of the subjects.

In recent years, I have become more aware of how I internalize ideas. This process will be different for you, but it is crucial to know what it is. The 3 Os framework is a great starting point for making better decisions, but it will be even more effective if you're able to integrate it in a "natural" way. To help you do that, let me go over some of the most relevant ideas in learning meta theory and how you can apply them to the 3 Os framework and much more.

Let's use language learning as our example since we all speak at least one language, and there's a high chance that you speak English. At some point in our lives, we learned the different building blocks of languages: verbs, subjects, prepositions, adverbs, and more. We also learned how to conjugate verbs in the present, past, and future. We can do all of this on the fly at the rate of speaking and writing. If you step back and think about it, that's quite amazing. I didn't fully appreciate it until I started learning Italian. I already knew Spanish and English, both of which I learned when I was a kid. I started learning Italian in my late twenties, a good 20 years after learning my first two languages.

Italian is quite similar to Spanish. In fact, it has a lexical value of 0.82 which means that these two languages share around 82% of words. The similarities made it easy for me to understand basic sentences and conversations. However, I had to learn the grammar from scratch. Grammar is complicated, and there are hundreds of rules followed by hundreds of exceptions. To internalize grammar, you need a combination of memorization and exposure. When we are kids, we are surrounded by the language we are learning, so we are easily exposed to thousands of hours in a short time.

Replicating this as an adult is trickier. I don't want you to have to spend thousands of hours before you can master the 3 Os framework, so let me share some ideas that you can apply today. You'll notice that you can actually use these ideas for any kind of learning.

Learning in Chunks

Our brain has a limited working capacity. The actual number is hotly debated, but we can test it ourselves with something as simple as a phone number. Memorizing six to nine digits is easy but going beyond that starts taxing our working memory. Unless we use mnemonic devices or something similar, we likely won't be able to remember multiple phone numbers.

When you learn new things, break them out in chunks. When I learn Italian, I learn a few words, conjugation, or go over previous chunks. When learning the 3 Os, take one step at a time. Practice working through outcomes or ranking the different options. Next time, you can go through a different chunk.

Numbers to Leave the Numbers

One of my favorite books on learning is *The Art of Learning* by Josh Waitzkin. In it, he talks about a concept called "numbers to leave the numbers." He is referring to chess in particular, but the spirit behind the concept is that you learn the rules so you can eventually discard them.

In the 3 Os framework, it is helpful to learn the relevant questions for each step so you can eventually discard them or replace them with your own questions. Even rephrasing the questions is part of this process.

Use Training Wheels

We all learned how to ride a bicycle using training wheels. If you didn't, email me because I would love to know a different approach. Training wheels are great because they provide stability while we learn how to pedal and stay upright. Eventually, we remove them and learn how to maintain balance while moving.

When learning the 3 Os framework, you can use the same concept. As you work through decisions, use notebooks or whiteboards to go through the steps. Print out worksheets that have important bullet points and questions that you can follow along. Get comfortable with the framework before you go for an unsupported ride.

Make Your Thought Process Visible

The fundamental goal of this chapter is to convert your "hidden" thinking process into something that is tangible. When using the 3 Os framework, keep this idea in mind. It may seem slower and tedious to have to write down the answers to the questions I provided, but this exposes your thinking. Seeing your thoughts on paper will make it easier to digest them and improve upon them.

BEHIND THE DECISION: UPS CEO SAYING NO

Going into 2020, United Parcel Service (UPS) was in a tricky position. In theory, their business should be well positioned for a future where e-commerce deliveries were increasing, and there was a higher demand for parcel deliveries. However, operating margins were failing at UPS, FedEx, and similar companies. They were dealing with infrastructure challenges and the constant pressure of prices.

Everything changed in March 2020 when COVID-19 shut down the entire world. One of the few things that didn't stop were package deliveries. In fact, it increased as more people moved to buying things online instead of going to physical stores. Among all the uncertainty, UPS appointed a new CEO, Carol Tome.

Fast forward one year to March 2021, and UPS is doing better. They have rode the pandemic successfully, and their stock price has nearly doubled. They are still working on the core infrastructure issues, but the first year has gone well for Ms. Tome.[*]

Part of her secret has been her ability to say "no." She wanted UPS to become more selective about the services they offered and the packages they delivered. She wants UPS to be "better, not bigger," a mantra which is reshaping the entire company. Her decision to focus on the best customers may be just what UPS needed in a bold new post-COVID-19 world.

UPS is a great example as to how one decision can impact hundreds and thousands of others. It also shows the power that a CEO can have on company morale and its prospects. Ms. Tome is bucking convention within UPS and pushing back against some of the culture rules. UPS is well known for rules like no left turns—which apparently are more likely to end up in accidents—seniority is king, and no sneakers.

I'm excited to see where UPS goes. Their focus on being paid fairly for their value, customer segmentation, and culture changes are fascinating to me. The first results from Ms. Tome's leadership style are paying off in a big way for UPS. We might just be watching a company go through rebirth in the middle of a global pandemic.

---

[*] "UPS Boss Preaches the Power of No," *Wall Street Journal*, accessed March 19, 2021, https://www.wsj.com/articles/ups-boss-preaches-the-power-of-no-11614335402

MAKING THE FRAMEWORK YOUR OWN

Bruce Lee once said, "Absorb what is useful, discard what is useless and add what is specifically your own." This is how I want you to approach the usage of the 3 Os framework. You know the steps, the questions at each step, and a few principles for learning it. It is time to think about how to make it your own. Think through the following questions to better understand this conversion process.

What steps resonate with you?

You may discover that you love the step of weighing options against an objective criterion, but you don't quite find the Outcomes step that useful. That's fine, take step 2 and blend it with your own decision-making process. Over time, you may discover that elements of step 1 are also useful, but it is more important to start using these ideas on a daily basis than to blindly accept them.

What steps come naturally or easy and what steps require work?

You also want to notice what steps come naturally and which steps require work. The natural steps are easier to digest and start using. That's great, take them and run with them. The steps that require work shouldn't be dismissed right away.

For example, you may struggle with the options step because you tend to think of options quickly. However, you may also choose options that tend to have issues in the long run. Getting comfortable with the weighing of options could be a game-changer in your decision-making process.

What else would you add to the framework?

I kept the framework simple because I loathe complexity. However, you may have another step that you would like to add. Perhaps you're interested in running ideas by your team, or you want to think about ways to leverage success within a decision. Whatever it may be, experiment with it. If you can find another step with the letter O, even better!

CHAPTER SUMMARY

- There are always going to be decisions that require a disciplined approach, and that's where the 3 Os framework comes in.
- There are three steps or components: Outcomes, Options, and Obstacles.
- Outcomes consist of the ideal scenario or future that you would like to achieve.
- Options are the different ways of getting there. Make sure to run options through certain objective criteria.
- Obstacles are the things that could get in the way of achieving your Outcomes. You can use the preventive and contingent ideas from Alan Weiss.
- Learn the framework through techniques like chunks, training wheels, and exposing your thought process.
- Make the framework your own by taking what is useful, rephrasing questions, and adding your own steps.

6

Knowing What's Best, When to Decide, and How to Tell Them Apart

In the small town of Clanton, Mississippi, Jake Brigance is a bold lawyer trying to make a living handling divorces, adoptions, and other small cases. That all changes when Jake is assigned to a capital murder case as the defense lawyer. The capital murder case involves killing a local police officer and puts Jake at odds with the whole town. What should Jake do?

The above is the main storyline from John Grisham's latest fictional novel, *No Time for Mercy*. Mr. Grisham is fantastic at fleshing out the details from even the most mundane aspects of legal practice. He has written over 40 books over the course of his career, and one of his most popular series is that of Jake Brigance, lawyer extraordinaire.

In the latest novel, Jake has to balance his duty as a defense lawyer with the practical realities of being involved in a controversial case. By pissing off the entire town where he lives, he risks alienating his entire customer base, all for a capital murder case where he will only get paid $1,000. The book delves into the moral conundrum and how it unfolds in unpredictable ways. Don't worry, I won't spoil the end of the book, but I highly recommend that you pick it up.

I was reminded of this book as I wrote this chapter because I wanted to dive into the more nuanced aspects of decision-making. In the next few chapters, we will look at morality, helping your team take ownership of their decisions, and how to trust your data in a world ruled by data. Consider the next few chapters the advanced version of what we have covered so far. In this chapter, I want to talk about judgment. We hear it in passing in phrases such as "you showed poor judgment" or "he had great

DOI: 10.4324/9781003185383-6

judgment during that play," but what does it really mean to have "good judgment"?

I belong to a social club in Vancouver with a private gym, private restaurant, and other amenities. One of my favorite activities at the club is monthly events called Lunch Exchanges, where we discuss topical ideas and issues. We had an entire series where we dove into ethics, morality, and similar topics. The very first thing we always had to do was to define what we meant by these words. As you can imagine, everyone had slightly different definitions of what it meant to be ethical or to do something that was morally correct.

The same thing can happen with judgment. Ask ten people, and you will get ten different definitions. With enough effort, I'm sure you can reconcile the differences and develop a global definition that satisfies almost everybody. For the context of this book, I have divided judgment into two broad categories: knowing what's best and knowing when to decide. The first category will look at how we determine the "best" or "right" decision. The second category will look at when we should decide and when we should let others decide. The second category is especially important for anyone who manages a team of any size.

Let's go back to John Grisham and Jake Brigance for one second. The law is a perfect example of why understanding judgment is important. There's a misconception that the law is black or white. You tend to hear this from certain political groups. You either broke the law, or you didn't. In reality, breaking the law isn't always enough to constitute a crime. This is why we have judges, juries, and lawyers who argue on the finer points of the law. If everything were black and white, we wouldn't need all these extra layers of information processing.

As a society, we have realized that we can't simply have a system that penalizes someone for a crime without allowing them to defend themselves. We even created distinctions for how to think about crimes. Murder can be categorized depending on intent and planning. If someone intends to kill someone and they plan for it, that is typically considered first-degree murder. If someone kills someone, but they didn't intend it, or it was an accident, that might be considered manslaughter. We use judgment to differentiate between these gray areas even if it is crystal clear that someone died.

Judgment is an intangible quality that shapes all our decisions. It is affected by our experience, our emotions, and how we think about decisions. Luckily for most of us, we don't have to regularly use our judgment to determine capital murder cases. However, we do have to learn to harness our judgment every day to make the right decisions. We also need to learn how to help our teams understand their judgment and cultivate it. Otherwise, we will always be stuck making the decisions for others.

I wish there was more focus on good uses of judgment, but it's a bad judgment that tends to stick out. At any given time, you can read about a politician who is being accused of corruption or a CEO who lied to their team and board of directors. As I write this, Andrew Cuomo, the current Governor of New York, is dealing with sexual harassment claims from multiple people.* It's unclear if his political career will survive this, but I bet he's looking back at instances where his judgment could have been better.

We can't avoid making mistakes, but we can avoid making the same mistakes repeatedly. By honing our judgment, we can start to unpack complex situations and understand the path forward. Instead of looking back and saying, "I wish I had said or done that," we can start to think about how these past decisions have shaped our judgment and our ability to make the right decisions.

KNOWING WHAT'S BEST

As I started writing this chapter, I realized that judgment was typically talked about as a "feeling" or "knowing what's right." People who said this seemed to know what good judgment was, but that didn't help me understand if my judgment was correct. Whenever we deal with ambiguous situations, the logical next step is to find ways to organize and add clarity. I can't say to a client that they should use "good judgment" without providing some tangible ideas on what this even means. In this section, I'll do my best to break out what the best decision (or outcome) should be.

---

* "Sexual Harassment Claims against Cuomo: What We Know So Far," *The New York Times,* accessed March 28, 2021, https://www.nytimes.com/article/cuomo-sexual-harassment-nursing-h omes-covid-19.html

There are four tactics that you can employ here. All four tactics involve running decisions through hypothetical situations to predict what might happen. If this sounds convoluted, don't worry about it. We actually already do this when we think about decisions. We'll naturally dream of how things might play out. As the basketball game starts, we imagine what it would feel like to win it. As we go on dates, we imagine what life would be like with this person. As we design new products, we imagine a successful launch and the accolades that follow that. You already do this all the time; we simply want to direct your efforts to uncover your judgment.

Tactic #1: Run through Consequences

The daydreaming scenarios I listed above tend to be mostly positive. Most of us lean toward positive outcomes, though I imagine that there's a group of people who default toward negative outcomes. The trouble with either approach in isolation is that we want to think about both of them together. We don't just have a rosy picture of everything going well. We want to know the best and worst case scenarios. To do that, we'll use the first tactic to think through the consequences of any given decision.

Let's take the example of how airlines are trying to bring back international travel. COVID-19 has caused historic drops in air travel, and it's unclear how airlines should adjust. Let's look at only one issue: should airlines force their employees to get the vaccine? Few developed countries make vaccines mandatory, though companies could impose their own restrictions. In this scenario, airline executives could run through the consequences of either decision (mandatory vaccines or optional).

In the mandatory case, there could be push back from the employees. Some of them might quit over this requirement. There could also be negative press as this information becomes public. Even if everyone is vaccinated, the risk of COVID-19 isn't zero, and there could still be cases among the employees. In the optional case, they could end up with an uneven vaccinated workforce. Employees and travelers could get sick, and that could generate negative press. We have seen cases where businesses had to shut down due to a handful of COVID-19 cases. A flight could easily generate hundreds of cases.

There are consequences on both sides of the decision. That's quite normal for complex situations and why we are even discussing judgment in this chapter. Based on the information above, what would you choose? Would you force your employees to be vaccinated, or would you let it be optional? You'll also notice that this kind of thinking is also the prelude to the preventive and contingent actions we spoke about in the chapter for the 3 Os framework. Anyway, back to judgment. Did you make a decision?

My take is that airlines should take the mandatory route. The number of employees who will push back will likely be small, as this is a profession that comes in contact with hundreds if not thousands of people in a short period of time. They spend a significant amount of time indoors, and it has been one of the most heavily affected industries. Anything that could help them get back in the air should be welcome. I also think the risk of travelers getting sick is too high. I would also advise the companies to run surveys and other studies to confirm these assumptions, but I would lean based on the information provided.

Tactic #2: Run Decision through a Moral Lens

The second tactic that we can employ is a moral lens. We touched on morality in a previous chapter on emotions, and we will dive deeper into it in an upcoming chapter. Morality is complex and veers into the philosophical. Nonetheless, we can still run a mental exercise trying to understand our moral stance and its decision.

Let's take another working example and imagine that you discover that one of your best employees is also dishonest. You manage a team of sales reps, and he is your best-performing rep over the past year. You just learned that he often plays loose with company expenses—taking personal friends on work lunches, claiming expenses that don't exist, and charging higher than normal rates for hotels and flights. You spoke with him about this, but little has changed since that conversation. What would you do here? Do you fire the employee or try to work through these issues?

Using a moral lens helps us go beyond what is most convenient into what is difficult but right. In the example above, I would lean toward letting go of the employee. While I would lose a significant chunk of sales, the impact on the rest of the team is higher. Other employees will think that this behavior is acceptable, and it might eventually affect clients if they discover that this is happening during visits or lunches.

Tactic #3: Run Decision through Different Preferences

The third tactic involves exploring different preferences. We all tend to have ways of doing things that work well but might differ from how others might do them. For example, we may have a system for managing files and folders. We developed it over the years, and we think it is efficient to find what you need quickly. The rest of the team might have different ways of organizing files. Do you force everyone to adopt your system, or do you find another solution?

In this mental exercise, we can explore what different preferences might look like. If everyone has their own way of handling files, what will happen? Can you impose a system for managing company files but let people manage their own files on their own? Is there a way to scale down your system, so it doesn't take years to learn?

It's important to understand when it is important to tackle a decision specifically because it is the most effective solution and when we simply have preferences for how things should be done. Anyone who has ever been micromanaged is effectively dealing with someone who can't let go of their preferences when tackling work. The micromanager might feel that other people cannot handle a task or have control issues. It doesn't matter; the outcome is the same.

There's an idiom that talks about "the hill you will die on." It refers to an issue that you will fight vigorously because you deeply care about it or think it is vitally important. I see too many executives die on the wrong hills. They have strong preferences, which they impose on their team even if their solution isn't the best. How files are organized, the order in which tasks are tackled, and how meetings are run are all examples of where preferences might differ. Be comfortable accepting other preferences and save your energy for the right hill.

Tactic #4: Run Decision through the Eyes of a Trusted Mentor or Someone You Look Up To

I'm currently watching *The Sopranos*, arguably one of the greatest TV shows of all time. The show is over 20 years old, but it still feels relevant even in 2021. One of the show's key themes is parenting and the example that characters like Tony Soprano (a mobster) sets for their children. Most of the children on the show tend to rebel against their parents in unexpected ways. We, as the viewers, can see that they are simply emulating how their Mafia parents act.

The fourth tactic is about using a similar idea. We all have mentors or people we look up to. It might even be your children or partner. As you think through a decision, think about what these people would think of your answer or solution. Would they be proud? Would they wonder why you're acting in a certain way? Is this a decision that you wouldn't want to share with them?

Sometimes we forget about the most important people in our lives and how they react to our decisions. The only reminder is that feeling of conflict in our bodies. We rationally made a choice, but our body isn't aligned with our mind. Be mindful of this conflict by trying to view your decision through the eyes of your most trusted friends and colleagues. You may realize that you need to make a different decision.

BEHIND THE DECISION: APPLE AND THE IPHONE

In 2007, Steve Jobs walked onto the stage at the Macworld convention and made an announcement that would change the world. There are few events that we can seriously apply under this category, but this one qualifies. Jobs talked about introducing a new device that could browse the web, play music, and make phone calls. He was talking about the first iPhone.

I still remember watching the presentation as a teenager. I loved technology, and watching Mr. Jobs use only his finger to play music seemed like magic. Like many people, I had a mobile phone. It was a Motorola Razr, a slim flip phone that I loved. However, it pales in comparison to the touchscreen iPhone. It took a few months, but I eventually got the first iPhone. The phone lived up to the hype, and I still remember it fondly.

The iPhone project had been underway within Apple under the banner of "Project Purple" for more than three years before its release. Apple knew that phones and music players would eventually mix under one device. Users were already carrying Blackberries and iPods, and it made sense to reduce the burden of users. To protect the iPod, Apple needed to release a phone that could do both.

Mr. Jobs also hated styluses and keyboards, the common way to operate phones at the time. The Blackberry was the phone of choice in the business world primarily because of the keyboard and overall security. The touchscreen technology was just coming to fruition, and Apple could take advantage of this trend. Eventually, the iPod got a touchscreen, and the iPad was released.

In the next few years, all phones would follow the same form factor: large touchscreen, rectangular size, and similar features. Even today, phones are quite similar to the original iPhone. Apple defined a new generation of devices, and everyone else eventually caught up. Today's phones are vastly more powerful than the original phone, and they play a crucial role in how we live. Most of us aren't very far from our phones at any point during the day.

Since its release in 2007, Apple has sold more than 1.5 billion worldwide and generated over $26.44 billion dollars. The market share for the iPhone is only around 10%, but it is one of the most profitable players in the space and for Apple. The iPhone has also allowed them to release other products like AirPods Pro and AirPods Max, wireless headphones that sync with the phone.

As a business decision, it's a home run. It checks all the boxes that you may want. Revenue goals, innovation, industry-defining, etc. It's important to see that Apple's decision was more a response to a growing trend than a drive to innovate for its own sake. They wanted to protect the moat of the iPod, and they thought that a phone would be the best way to do that. Touchscreen phones already existed, and it was becoming increasingly clear that phones were becoming more important to consumers. Apple wasn't trying to invent a trend, simply jump on one.

KNOWING WHEN TO DECIDE

The second aspect of the judgment is knowing when to decide and when to let someone else do it. Executives are constantly telling me that they feel frustrated that their team isn't showing enough initiative and ownership over critical decisions. They feel that they have to handhold their team members through even the smallest of decisions, limiting their ability to tackle big decisions. They don't want to micromanage, but it seems like they have no choice.

Letting other people make decisions that affect us can be scary. We may lose our feeling and our control, or we may find it difficult to see someone make the wrong decisions when we know, without a shadow of a doubt, that right decision. Despite all of this, by letting go of this desire to make the right decisions, we can help people even more. Everything in this book has been about helping you get to the right outcome. Frameworks, problem-solving, and strategies to get you to the right answer. As we dive into judgment, we start to realize that there are bigger goals than getting a decision right.

There's also a vicious cycle that can be created here. If we make the decisions for someone, that person may come to rely on us all the time. Instead of creating an independent individual capable of critical thinking and decisiveness, we create a codependent relationship. This dynamic exists at work and on a personal level. You don't want codependent employees who merely execute what you tell them to do. You want people who own their decisions and make progress without constant prodding. The same is true for personal relationships. You want your children to feel comfortable making their own decisions—and mistakes.

There's a lot of talk about the rising dominance of China. The Chinese government runs a hybrid model of communism and capitalism that seems to take the best elements of each model. Mr. Jinping, the current president of China, has ruled China since 2013. In that time, millions of people have escaped poverty, moved to the cities, and helped create some of the most dominant companies in the world. China is always executing five-year plans, and there's little doubt that it will continue to grow and exert its global influence.

Putting aside any criticisms of China—of which they are many—their government is growing increasingly authoritarian. Mr. Jinping has worked to remove opposition, and there's a growing trend of trying to appease the government even if that isn't the best decision. The trouble with this approach is that eventually, it backfires. People withhold information that leads to serious issues. There's some evidence that the COVID-19 wasn't fully communicated during the early stages because provincial governments were afraid of the response by the national government. Co-dependent relationships severely impact decision-making, and avoiding it is the key to long-term success.

I want to give you four questions to ponder whenever you come across a decision that could be made by someone else. Like everything else in this book, questions are training wheels that you will eventually get rid of. You can then internalize them and run through them to understand if a decision is for you.

1. Is there an opportunity for learning?

Rookie basketball players tend to go through an "awakening" period when they first join the NBA. These players have typically dominated through most of their childhood and high school teams, usually through their pure talent. When they join the NBA, they find themselves surrounded by people just as talented as them, older, stronger, and wiser. The adjustment is tough, and not all rookies make it. The best players accept that they will have to lose for years before getting the chance to win again. LeBron James didn't win his first championship until eight years after joining the league, and he didn't even make the finals until four years after joining.

When facing a decision, think about the potential opportunities for learning for other people. If you decide for them, you are depriving them of this learning. It would be like NBA teams avoiding playing rookies because they will miss their shots. There's a good chance that rookies will not play as well, and they might even be a hindrance for their team, but they need to get experience if they are ever to get good. Your team members might make the wrong decisions initially, but that's how they will learn to make the right ones. Learning is burned into our minds when we have ownership over the mistake or success. It's hard to learn vicariously through others.

2. Should someone else be taking ownership?

I worked with a client where the CEO was heavily involved in the day-to-day projects. I was amazed at how much he knew about what was happening in any given project. In a way, this CEO was acutely aware of what customers wanted and how their team was performing. In another way, the CEO was too involved. I kept seeing the rest of his team wait for him to tell them what to do. He wasn't doing a good job of letting his team make mistakes and take ownership of their decisions. Privately, he was frustrated, but he was part of the problem.

I have met people who have a huge desire to help others. They constantly find themselves taking ownership over decisions that shouldn't concern them. Not every problem and decision is your duty to solve. We sometimes need to let people work through decisions, regardless of the outcome. As you face decisions, pause and reflect on who should truly own it. It's not a question about whether you have the ability to do it but if you should. I will also note the role of ego here. Wanting to help people can be blurred by ego and thinking that only we could help this person or this decision. If no one else does it, then I will. Be mindful of what decisions you're taking on because you think you're the most qualified person in the room. You might be limiting the growth of others.

3. Is there any irreversible harm in making the wrong decision?

Letting go of decisions sounds easy in theory. The reality can be much tougher to stomach. One of the criteria that can help you delegate decisions is irreversible harm. That is if someone makes the wrong decision, is the damage permanent? You might discover that in most situations, the answer is no. I know what you will say. You will point to all the exceptions that prove the rule false. I said most situations, and I would also challenge myself to think through what it means to have permanent damage.

Parents often struggle to guide their children through the tricky teenage years. Drinking is one of the issues that come up during this period. As a teenager, I didn't drink much myself. I never quite picked up a taste for alcohol, but I did have a couple of experiences where I drank too much, and my parents found out. I can imagine that my parents felt frustrated at my poor decisions, but as it turns out, these were learning experiences, and they weren't permanent. We can't make decisions for others because we are protecting against an unlikely but damaging possibility. The same applies to your team. Make a distinction between permanent and temporary damage and think through how you could recover from even the worst decisions.

4. Is this decision going to occur again in the future?

The possibility of a recurring decision is another criterion to think about. If a decision is bound to occur in the future, there is a greater argument for letting others make it. If your team needs your approval before launching a new campaign or launching a feature, you might become the bottleneck in the entire process. It would be more effective to work with others to help them understand when something is ready to go live. The initial work to delegate the decision will pay itself back multiple times over the long run.

Don't take common events and assume that they always need your blessing or insight. One-off events like COVID-19 are rare. I can imagine that executive teams were forced to make decisions that no one else could make in their companies. They had to rely on little data to make some of the toughest decisions their company might ever face. If they didn't delegate these decisions, I understand. However, don't treat regular situations—good or bad—as rare events that no one could have predicted. By letting go, you can move on to other things where your insight could be even more impactful.

HOW THE CONTEXT CHANGES SITUATIONS

Context changes everything. Saying "Uh oh, there's a problem" while you're cooking is vastly different from hearing it from the pilot while you're flying. Part of judgment understands the subtleties of making decisions in different situations. There's a wide range of lessons that we only pick up by seeing them manifest in different circumstances. For example, think about teenagers in high school and how they learn the different social rules that will govern the rest of their lives. They'll get an intuitive feeling for when they can say certain things and when they should keep their mouths shut.

There are three areas that I would like to explore when it comes to context. You can think of them as three dimensions that could significantly alter how your approach any given decision. You should also be aware of how any of these dimensions could make simple decisions difficult to make. Read on to understand the three areas: personal, assumptive and urgent. As with everything, there might be a few other ones, but I think these are the most important and common.

Personal

The Personal dimension refers to anything that will affect you, your family, or close ones. Once something becomes personal, it can become harder to make objective decisions. The emotional element ramps up to 11, and we may find it trickier to sort through all the variables available to us.

Think about what happens when a friend asks you for advice. Everything seems so clear, and the solution is obvious. Your friend is clearly not seeing or choosing not to see it. However, if the same problem would affect us, things wouldn't be as clear. The situation might be identical, but there's now an undertone of uncertainty once it involves us directly.

Let's look at another example from work. Imagine that you're getting complaints about an underperforming employee in your team. The performance has been lacking for months now, and the evidence is clear. You have talked to this person multiple times about the lackluster performance, but there have been few improvements. However, the employee happens to be your cousin, who you also see in family situations every month. What would you do? How do you handle the potential fallout from any decision?

Some might think that you would never find yourself in this position because you don't hire family members or close friends. Put that aside for a second and think through the scenario. I design the scenario to have a limited number of outcomes for simplicity's sake. We can't go back and talk to the cousin because we already did that. It didn't work. We are now faced with drastic choices, such as letting the person go. In my opinion, I would advise firing the person and let him or her go. They are clearly not doing well at this job, but that doesn't mean that they won't do well at another job. It might just be a poor fit. Keeping them employed would hurt them more in the long run because their confidence might take a hit, or they might come to believe that they can't do anything properly.

There might be issues with the family. Being honest about why this is taking place and offering to help (outside of work) find another job could help smooth things out. Dealing with people who aren't happy with your decision is unavoidable. You also have to think about the greater performance of your team. Seeing favoritism can plant seeds of resentment, especially if it's obvious that it isn't based on merit. This scenario is a good example of how the Personal dimension makes decisions harder. You may need to deal with strong feelings of fear, uncertainty, and anger as you make these decisions.

Assumptive

Assumptions are the second dimension that can poison or elevate decisions. We all have assumptions as to what might happen. They can be minor, such as how much traffic you will hit on your way home, or they can be major, such as how your daughter will perform in an upcoming math exam. One of my favorite teachers told us that we all wear rose-colored glasses, which shape our worldview. In today's language, you might say that we all look at the world through a specific Instagram filter. Assumptions are the filter or glasses, and things can come across wildly different behind these lenses.

Assumptions become relevant because of their potential impact on the outcome of decisions. If we expect someone to fail at something, that expectation will show in some shape or form. It might come across in the specific words or tone that you use when you discuss this idea. Carol Dweck is a psychologist who studies motivation, especially in children. She wrote a fantastic book called *Mindset: The New Psychology of Success*, where she talks about the fixed vs growth mindset. The fixed mindset states that your abilities are inherently limited. If you're not good at math, then there isn't anything you can do to improve that. The growth mindset states that you can learn new skills and abilities if you apply yourself.

These ideas have been around in psychology for a long time, but Ms. Dweck focuses on how children learn them. As it turns out, children will develop one of these two mindsets, which will match their parent's mindset. When a child does well in math, a parent can reinforce the fixed or the growth mindset. The fixed mindset is reinforced by saying things like, "you were clearly born to be good at math like your mom." The growth mindset is reinforced by saying, "you worked hard to understand these concepts, good job!" You can also see the flipside played out whenever children are told that "they aren't cut out for sports" or "your mom isn't good at math, which is why you aren't." Behind these two concepts, we see the power of our own assumptions.

In your team, you also need to watch out for assumptions. Expecting your team to fail or expecting a team member to be late with their work can be disastrous. If things go sideways, you will feel that you were right and can't trust your team. If things go well, you might think that your team got lucky. Everyone tends to live up to their expectations, which is why leaders need to set the right example and manage their assumptions. If you have negative assumptions, then keep them to yourself as much as possible. Focus on tangible evidence and remember that the past isn't a good predictor of the future.

Urgent

The third dimension revolves around urgency. If you had all the time in the world, you could think through decisions, delegate them, and everything would be mostly fine. The reality is that we operate in tight timelines. Campaigns need to be launched this week. Customer surveys have to go out by Monday, or prospects need to be called back within 24 hours. Urgency forces us to make certain decisions because "we have to" or "there's no time to do it that way." The key to handling this dimension is to recognize true urgency from artificial.

I live a few blocks from St. Paul's hospital, the main hospital in downtown Vancouver. Every day, there are ambulances that go by my building, and it tends to increase during the weekends. Every time I hear an ambulance, I'm reminded of what true urgency feels like. The ambulance might pick someone up who could be in a life or death struggle, or they may be driving back with someone who is severely ill and needs immediate assistance.

I don't deny that businesses—which aren't hospitals—also experience urgency in their work. However, I am skeptical whenever I see what I considered artificial urgency. Your company may operate like this, or you may have worked in a company that did. These are the companies where everything is due ASAP, calls are needed on the weekend to get ready for Monday morning, or things always seem to be running late, and hence, an urgent push is needed. If you're in that kind of environment, it can be difficult to use any of the techniques in this book because you're always putting out fires.

This book isn't focused on how to change company cultures, but I do think the culture of artificial urgency is overall inefficient. By always rushing through things, mistakes are made. People aren't able to properly assess what might be needed, and there's a large amount of failure work— any work where something has to be repeated. If you're in charge of a team, you should make a serious effort to use urgency only when necessary. Adding urgency to every day of work is bound to limit what you can actually do. You'll be walking around thinking that everything is falling apart instead of looking for opportunities for growth and innovation.

BEHIND THE DECISION: INVASION OF NORMANDY

In 1943, the war in Europe was turning against Nazi Germany. The Allies had launched an invasion of Sicily in July 1943, and Soviet forces were in control after winning the Battle of Stalingrad. The Allies had decided to undertake a cross-channel invasion from Britain into the European mainland. The task wasn't going to be easy.

After careful consideration, the Allies decided to land in Normandy. It would require significant investment in building ports and troops, but they thought it would be their best chance at building momentum toward an eventual invasion of Berlin and the surrender of the Nazis. By the time the plan was finalized, over a million troops were scheduled to be part of the offensive.

The landing of troops in Normandy is perhaps best captured by *Saving Private Ryan*, the Spielberg film. It shows the harrowing moments as troops land on the beaches and try to establish themselves without being killed by the German defenses. These landings were the largest seaborne invasion in history. Allies casualties on the first day were around 10,000 while the Germans lost around 1,000 men. Allies would continue to move inland and eventually win the war in 1945. The rest, as they say, is history.*

D-Day is one of the pivotal points in WWII. It was the result of meticulous planning and bold action. I can't even fathom what it was like to be part of the operation, whether on the frontlines or in the planning stages. The defeat in Normandy was a significant psychological blow to the Nazis, and it was the start of the end.

The decision to undertake this plan and the hundreds, if not thousands of decisions that had to be made are staggering. The Allies took hard-earned lessons from other initiatives and used them in Normandy. Normandy wasn't the last battle in the war, but it set up a second front and became a key strategic point in the war.

In hindsight, we know that this decision was incredibly effective. It wasn't perfect, but it served the appropriate role at this point in the war. The execution of the decision was also quite good, and the Allies' commanders adjusted well to the rapidly changing conditions on the ground. The success and sacrifices made during D-Day are one of the major points to remember during holidays like Remembrance Day worldwide.

---

* "D-Day and the Battle of Normandy," The Canadian Encyclopedia, accessed April 1, 2021, https://www.thecanadianencyclopedia.ca/en/article/normandy-invasion

APPLYING THE THREE STRATEGIES IN A RAPIDLY CHANGING WORLD

We covered three strategies for dealing with decisions in previous chapters. The judgment allows you to determine when you should use each strategy and when you skip them altogether. If you have ever played or learned chess, you will be familiar with the basic rules of moving pawns, knights, and bishops. As you go deeper into the game theory, you realize that all the rules of how to move pieces properly—such as not moving your queen too early—have exceptions. Your knowledge is built on fundamentals which are then supplemented by edge cases. The same applies to how judgment is used in the real world.

One of the constant sayings in the business world today is that things are changing rapidly. Companies used to define strategy for five years or beyond. That is now seen as ludicrous, and one-to-three-year timelines are becoming more common. Some companies are going further and setting a strategic goal and planning for the next 12 months. There is some truth to the idea that conditions change quickly. Putting COVID-19 aside, we have seen massive consumer behavior changes in the last 20 years alone. The introduction of smartphones, the availability of high-speed internet, the rise of social media, the dissolution of the family dinner, and the reduction in religious affiliation are some of these changes.

I can't tell you what will happen in the next few years. Like other experts in the world, I can make predictions based on my experience but be wary of anyone who claims a definite understanding of the future. Crazy ideas can seem like gospel in hindsight, but it is easy to forget all the times we were wrong. You sometimes see this with cult-like churches which talk about the end of the world. They will talk about the final days for years— and perhaps one day they will be right—but that doesn't mean that we can ignore all the hundreds or thousands of times they were wrong.

Instead, you should think about how to develop skills and systems to deal with anything. The strategies I covered in the previous chapters are helpful in good times but essential in turbulent times. Like soldiers are trained to unconsciously rely on their training during the war, we can train ourselves to fall back on strategies for dealing with uncertainty and change. Archilochus once said that "we don't rise to the level of our expectations, we fall to the level of our training." If you're having issues solving when things are stable, it will be even more difficult while in movement.

The first strategy was problem-solving. The idea is that before you get moving on anything, you should spend time determining what direction you should take. Wasted energy toward the wrong outcome is what we are trying to avoid. In rapidly changing conditions, problem-solving gets trickier because you will face less information and a higher level of urgency. Imagine executives that had to decide how to convert their companies into remote-friendly work environments within days or weeks in early 2020.

I would recommend that you do your best to maintain some kind of problem-solving process in the plan. You can reduce the steps and compress them. What might have taken you one week, you might now need to do in one day. You'll be forced to work on assumptions, but you can still think about what might go wrong, how you can fix it, and how to avoid going down rabbit holes. It's also important to manage your main driving force. Emotions will be running high during these situations, and it can be easy to let them drive your decision-making. I don't expect you to suppress your emotions but instead balance them out with a checklist of sorts.

The second strategy was routines or the Turtleneck Principle. I think routines are the most undervalued strategy during turbulent times. When things get hectic, we can fall into downward spirals. I was speaking with an executive who was telling me about an upcoming product launch. It was a significant milestone for the company, and everyone was working long hours—and weekends. She admitted that the pressure was cutting into her family time, her ability to work out, her eating habits, and her sleep. All of this made the pressure even worse. It's hard enough to deal with this kind of challenge, imagine doing that while sleep-deprived, sluggish, and dealing with personal issues.

Routines should be seen as even more important during these times. Your gym appointments, your personal time, and your sleep are all examples of things that should be protected. They may feel like a luxury, but you can also see them as support that prevents things from getting worse. If you're truly pressed for time, you could reduce their commitment. Instead of going to the gym for 90 minutes, you might go for only 45. We all have to compromise, but don't assume that you have to give everything up for short-term goals—things that have to consume your entire life for them to be worthwhile.

The third strategy is the 3 Os. Just like problem-solving, uncertainty makes this framework even more valuable. Hard framework decisions can become harder if you don't have a series of steps for getting to the best answer. You still need to make the decision, and you might not be happy with the options, but at least you can weigh them and run them through some criteria. Even if you only use some of the steps—option ranking or obstacle thinking, for example—you will be better off than you would be trying to hold on to water as it slips through your fingers.

Decisions made during these times can also reverberate for years. Look at how Nike is reacting to the pandemic. Since they had a strong brand, they did relatively well despite the lockdowns. However, Nike realized that they should improve their connection to the customer. They are now moving to become a DTC (Direct to Consumer) brand instead of primarily selling through partners like Foot Locker. These kinds of strategic decisions have significant repercussions, and you will be forced to make similar ones during the toughest times.

Judgment is tricky to pin down. I have done my best to flesh it out and give you something to hold on to. Run through the questions and become more familiar with how your judgment works and how it operates during uncertain times. Improving our judgment is one of the best investments we can all make. It's one of the few things that AI and computers will struggle to ever replace, and no one can make decisions for us. Most of the challenges we face fall within our control in some way. This is good and bad: good because we can influence outcomes in a positive way and bad because we can influence them—but we can also procrastinate. As Richard Feynman once said, "The first principle is that you must not fool yourself and you are the easiest person to fool."

CHAPTER SUMMARY

- Judgment is the underlying set of principles that govern all of our decisions.
- Learn how to know what is best and when you should decide. You don't always need to make a decision yourself, and there are always multiple outcomes possible.
- Know what's best by running through consequences, using a moral lens, analyzing different preferences, or leveraging a trusted advisor.

- When delegating decisions, think about opportunities for learning, ownership, avoiding irreversible damage, and recurring decisions.
- Context changes everything. Remember that context can be seen in three dimensions: Personal, Assumptive, and Urgent.
- The three strategies we covered so far are even more important during rapidly changing conditions.

7

How Leaders Make Decisions in Tough Situations

It all started with a blog post.* The post introduced new policies at a company called Basecamp (formerly known as 37Signals), a software company. The policies seemed logical. No more politics at work, no more committees, no more 360 reviews, and a couple of other ones. The most important change, though, was centered around politics. There were to be no more conversations on company time around highly charged topics like racism or societal issues. I don't think anyone expected the kind of backlash that this post would have.

Over the next few days, things hit the fan. Basecamp is a small company of around 60 employees at the time of publishing this blog post. However, they are highly influential in the world of technology and startups. They are known for provocative ideas about running a company that they have talked about in books like *Rework*, *It Doesn't Have to Be Crazy at Work*, and *Remote: Office Not Required*. They have created one of the strongest company cultures and consistently attracted top talent. They have also been in business for 20+ years.

That blog post was posted on April 26. By May 4, an estimated 40% of the company had quit Basecamp. That meant around 30 employees left a 60-person company. Entire teams such as their iOS department quit. What happened? How do you go from a seemingly "normal" company update to a significant employee exodus? The story isn't as clear as you might expect,

---

* "Basecamp Implodes as Employees Flee Company, Including Senior Staff," The Verge, accessed April 30, 2021, https://www.theverge.com/2021/4/30/22412714/basecamp-employees-memo-po licy-hansson-fried-controversy

DOI: 10.4324/9781003185383-7

but it did play out in the media. Since Basecamp is so well known, multiple outlets covered the unfolding drama and got inside scoops into meetings.

After the blog post went live, there was immediate backlash. It seems that the company had recently been talking about diversity. There was a committee formed in which half the company joined. The committee found a document that had captured funny-sounding customer names. Basecamp has a global audience. Someone had decided to start this list which the committee felt was discrimination. The list had been around for some time, and no one seemed to have done anything about it.

When it was brought up to leadership's attention, it seems like the response wasn't appropriate. The list was dismissed, and it started an entire conversation which led to the blog post. After the post went live, the company held an all-hands meeting to discuss it. The conversation got heated and delved into topics of white supremacy, racism, and diversity. Employees felt that they were being ignored, and the new rules were meant to suppress any dissent. Leadership wanted to focus on running a business, and they thought that the new policies would prevent conflicts among their team.

Basecamp decided to offer generous severance packages to anyone who disagreed with the new policies. Six months of salary were offered to long-time employees and three months to newer ones. The generous package likely contributed to the exodus, as it was a significant amount of money. Many employees were also highly sought as they were mobile developers, UX designers, and data scientists. However, it wasn't just money that led people to leave. They were legitimately unhappy with the new direction and what it foreshadowed in the future.

Many things went wrong in this situation, and it was likely made worse by how the leadership team responded. We can't know the exact causes of the crises, but it seems that it goes back to the list of funny-sounding names and how they responded. That then snowballed into a broader topic around politics. Things are already highly polarized in the United States, and I don't think you could have a conversation around politics without things getting emotional. Some of the comments from the all-hands meeting showed that people were put in impossible positions.

Leadership is a tough business. You have to deal with different opinions, personalities, and ideas, all while trying to get everyone to move in a specific direction. The Basecamp example shows how tricky leadership can be. How do you deal with huge societal issues like racism within your own company? Do you need special qualifications or training? The answers aren't as clear. The same words may be interpreted differently based on how you behaved in the past or even the tone you use.

In this chapter, we will look at how the world of leadership interconnects with decision-making. As you go higher in an organization, you will find yourself doing less hands-on work and making more decisions. You will decide on how budgets are allocated, who gets hired, or what strategy to follow. Having different tools to tackle tough decisions is invaluable. We have talked about frameworks like the 3 Os, but I want to share a few other ways of thinking about decisions.

KNOWING WHEN TO INVOLVE YOUR TEAM IN DECISIONS

The study of leadership has fascinated researchers for over 50 years. It can be traced back to the origins of management as we know it today. Frederick Winslow Taylor thought that manufacturing operations could be made more efficient if you could just measure everything. He would ask workers to move rocks while he timed them to determine an average. His work eventually evolved into the "Big Idea" man: Peter Drucker. Drucker wrote about innovation, leadership, and how to build companies.

In leadership, one of my favorite books is aptly called *Leadership and Decision-Making* by Victor H. Vroom and Phillip W. Yetton. It was written in 1973, and it looks at the research around how decisions are made in a corporate environment. It boils down to one major question: when should you involve others in a decision? The nuances will be apparent to any executive. Should you involve your team in strategy? What about personnel decisions, including hiring and firing? Should everyone have a say in the budget?

Vroom and Yetton build a model that looks at three major decisions: authoritative, consultative, or collaborative. They provide guidelines for thinking about decisions and the criteria that would be required for each one. All in all, it's a deep look at a complex topic. Based on their ideas and my work, I created a simplified model that shows a different approach to tackling the same issues. My model also has three types of decisions, and I also created four criteria to determine which one you should choose (Figure 7.1).

Leadership Decision-Making Matrix

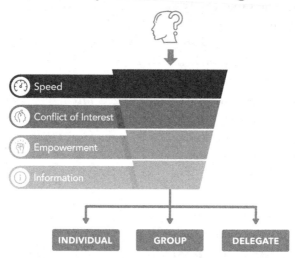

FIGURE 7.1
Leadership Decision-Making Matrix (LDMM)

The three types of decisions in my LDMM (Leadership Decision-Making Matrix) are as follows:

1. Individual: You + Info
2. Group: You + Others
3. Delegate: Others

Let's unpack this model. You always have options when it comes to making any decision. The first type is simply you deciding on your own. You might need to look for supporting information which could be external in the form of documents or internal in the form of your thoughts. Either way, you will weigh all the evidence and make the final decision yourself. Many leaders feel like all their most important decisions fall into this category. They are carrying the "weight" of their companies every time they make a decision.

The second type is when you involve others in the decision-making process. You could ask a colleague or someone in your team for their opinion on the decision, or you could formally gather multiple people in a room to discuss the decision. At the end of the discussion, you may decide to decide yourself or let the group decide. Group decisions can be great for getting buy-in and ensuring key opinions are considered. They can also be a disaster depending on what is being decided.

The third type is when you delegate the decision to others. In this type, you remove yourself completely from the decision-making process. You will support whatever decision is made by those who you appoint to explore it. Delegation is the key to have a sane work-life as an executive, but not enough of them are doing this. It's also important to note that delegation can backfire if the people appointed don't have the necessary skills or information to decide.

The three types of decisions are then weighed through four criteria:

- Speed
- Empowerment
- Conflict of Interest
- Information

You can likely imagine how each of these criteria fits into the three types of decisions. Individual decisions have a high speed while Group decisions are slower, and Delegate decisions are the slowest. If you need to make a fast decision, you might be better off doing it yourself. Watch out for tricky situations, though. I once worked with an executive who intuitively understood the speed criterion, but he defaulted too much to speed. He was making too many decisions and preventing his team from growing and being more accountable. Speed is important, but it's not the only criterion.

The second aspect to consider is empowerment. I talked previously about this phrase, but it simply means encouraging your team or colleagues to take ownership of their work. The CEO in the previous example did not score well on the empowerment scale. Individual decisions have low empowerment, Group decisions have higher empowerment, and Delegated decisions have the highest value. There are decisions where it is worth sacrificing speed to achieve higher empowerment. Speed is also something that could increase in the future if you're able to trust and train your team.

The third aspect is a conflict of interest. If you're thinking of making personnel changes, it will be difficult to let your team make these decisions. Their conflict of interest is too high, and you will need to rely on a more Individual decision model. On the other hand, a decision to determine the next round of marketing campaigns might have a low conflict of interest, which can easily fit into the Delegate model. Once again, trust is behind all decisions. In some companies, trust needs to be calibrated to avoid seeing everyone as biased.

The fourth and final aspect is information. You can't ask a manager to determine the strategy for the company because he or she will likely lack information. They will not know all the intricacies of what the company is doing and how it needs to be positioned in the future. In this case, their information is low, and you will need to rely on a Group decision model or perhaps an Individual one. Some companies like Netflix share everything among employees. In their world, information isn't an issue, and this allows them to rely more on Delegation to make even the critical decisions of buying a TV show. Your mileage may vary, as they say.

Now that we have the three decision types and the four models, we can see how past decisions worked and didn't work. You may discover that you took on too many decisions that could have easily fit in the Group or Delegate model. Perhaps you tried to make decisions using an Individual model, but you didn't have enough information. Or you tried to Delegate decisions, but your team's conflict of interest was high, or they didn't have the required information to make those decisions.

The beauty of this model is that we can begin to slice decisions into tangible areas for improvement. Saying that team members "aren't able to make their own decisions" isn't very helpful. Do they lack information? Have they been given a chance to contribute to decisions in a Group model? Is enough Delegation taking place? These are the questions that we can start to think about to improve our leadership approach to decision-making. You don't have to carry the weight of your company on your shoulders. There are countless decisions where you can get the correct support and perhaps even delegate completely. It's also worth exploring external sources of support such as peer groups, accountability partners, and even therapy.

I hope that the LDMM also shows you that you can't make all the decisions yourself. There is not enough time to learn everything that could be required. You do need to lean on others, whether in a Group or Delegation format. Many executives have realized that many of the most effective solutions to problems tend to come from those closest to the actual problem. An engineer might have the solution to a tricky problem and could share it if only the management team had a process for doing that.

BRINGING ETHICS AND MORALS INTO
THE 21ST-CENTURY ORGANIZATION

In the middle of WWII, there was a philosophical debate on how to approach bombing. The British RAF believed in area bombing. The American Air Force believed in precision bombing. Area bombing raids were done at night, which was safer. You would simply drop bombs over an area that includes military targets and civilians. The goal was to defeat the enemy by breaking the spirit of their people. Precision bombing was the opposite. The thesis was that if you could hit critical targets, you might be able to stop or slow down the enemy's war machine. Destroying all of their ball bearings factories could be enough to gain an advantage in the deadly art of war.

The problem with precision bombing is that it wasn't as easy as area bombing. Technology didn't exist that would allow precision bombing in the way we see it today. Carl Norden developed the Norden Bombsight to determine how to drop a bomb from 20,000 feet in the air and hit a factory. The problem is trickier than you can imagine. The Norden Bombsight utilized 64 algorithms to spit out the exact moment when a bomb should be dropped. One of the algorithms even considered how much the earth would rotate on its axis while the bomb dropped to the ground. In the 30 seconds that it would take the bomb to hit, the earth would rotate a few feet. The algorithm had to account for that.

Area bombing was being used by the Nazis as well. They famously bombed London for 42 days straight. It was clear that it wasn't just about hitting military targets but about killing civilians. How could the allies do precision bombing when their enemy was destroying their cities? The area bombing group eventually won the argument. The allies would go on to bomb German cities like Dresden and Berlin. However, area bombing would be perfected not in Europe but the Pacific theater.

In the last year of the war, the allies were conflicted about how to deal with Japan. The Japanese seemed unwilling to surrender and felt that a land invasion would prove costly to the allies in terms of lives. Around this time, Napalm was created by accident. Scientists were shocked at how effective it was at burning everything it touched. The Allies realized that most of the Japanese cities were constructed with wood and were highly flammable. A city like Osaka was estimated to be 80% flammable. The first major test of Napalm was done in Tokyo. The results were staggering. It is estimated that more people died in a six-hour period in Tokyo after the bombing than ever before in history. Over 100,000 people would die from the first attack.

The Allies would go on to attack 67 cities in Japan with Napalm. In some cities, the burning would consume upwards of 70% of the city. Precision bombing was dead, and area bombing was the way to go by this point in the war. Deciding to drop the atomic bombs was an evolution from the firebombing that was taking place. The bombs dropped on Hiroshima and Nagasaki ended WWII, but our questions about these actions' morality are still being debated today. It wasn't just the atomic bomb that had to be questioned. The effectiveness of Napalm and its use in Japan has raised serious questions.

The morality of war is tough for us to comprehend. We live in one of the most peaceful times in history, and it's hard for some to fathom what war was like. I personally grew up in a crime-ridden country, but that's not the same as war. Instead, our moral conversations center around societal issues like diversity, politics, and climate change. Companies today aren't asked to join the war effort but are being asked to establish policies that will help the world. What should be your company's role in local events? Should you get involved in national controversies? What do you do if your employees want your company to take a stand?

These are the questions that every executive and leader is asking themselves. The Economist ran an issue titled "The Political CEO," where it looked at the increasing role of companies in political conversations. Companies like Nike aren't staying silent on issues. They are actively running ads promoting their stance. Delta offered to fly the body of George Floyd back to his family. Chick-Fil-A is actively telling customers what they believe and who should be buying their fast food products. Customers see these companies take a stand and then expect all companies to do the same.

The data on these actions isn't strong. Boycotts of a company tend to stick in the minds of a consumer, but consumers actively choosing to work with a company because what they said or did doesn't seem to show in the data. In other words, consumers will stop using your products out of boycotts but are unlikely to start buying your products to support your stands. However, this might be an issue. Morality isn't just about profit. It's about following principles regardless of the outcome.

That being said, here are a few trends that you should be aware of. Our conversation, ethics, and morals take place within our world and how we see the world. There's an inclination to judge the past based on our current morals—aptly called presentism—but that's not with the scope of this chapter. As an executive and leader, you need to make ethical and moral decisions today and for the future, not for the past.

Trend #1: Limited Avenues to Express Ideas

Political conversations have become especially charged in recent years, and you might think they are taking place all the time. In reality, I believe that we have fewer outlets to talk about politics today. People recoil from discussing it with friends and family out of fear of conflict. They avoid online channels like social media due to a large amount of hate and trolls. We belong to fewer community groups like churches. This naturally leaves work as a potential place for discussion. There's an expectation that our colleagues at work would be professional and would listen to our opinions. Conflicts naturally happen at work, and we spend a significant portion of our time working.

As a leader, this puts you in a tricky position. People want to express their positions and expect companies to do the same. You might have a diverse customer base, or you very likely have a diverse workforce. I'm not sure if work is even the right place for these kinds of discussions. Our example of Basecamp showed how things could backfire. On the other hand, other companies make it work. You will likely have to experiment and see how this plays out within your individual culture. Be aware of the ongoing pressure for people to merge multiple identities instead of isolating parts of their lives.

Trend #2: People Want to Support Causes They Care about

Consumers now have way more choices than before. They are also acutely aware of how products get made and their impact on their lives. Naturally, we now have a growing segment of consumers who don't simply want to buy products, they also want to support companies that align with their values. You don't just want to buy meat; you want to support local farmers. You don't just want electric cars; you want to do your part for climate change.

Companies can fall into impossible conversations if they lean too heavily into causes. Electric cars may appeal to people who aren't as concerned about the environment. Choosing to alienate them may prove costly. We can also see that the minority tends to be quite vocal, and you might think that all consumers feel a certain way about a certain cause. In reality, you may see that things aren't as clear-cut. You can find ways to tap into strong emotions and causes, but be careful that you don't get swept up in the river's force.

Trend #3: Amplification of Mistakes

The world of social media and digital channels amplifies everything to 100. You hear the latest news morphed through biases. Rumors can snowball into mainstream news. Someone heard or read about something on Twitter, and now it is being reported as news. When the pandemic started, there was a rumor that the Canadian government was going to shut down grocery stores. Suddenly, people rushed to the stores at 11pm to buy things before the impending shutdown. The closing of stores never actually took place.

Executives fear saying the wrong thing. It will get shared and amplified through social media in a way that may come across as worse than it really is. Worse of all, everything happens rapidly. Before you know it, your comments have been turned into memes, and you're receiving death threats from strangers. Be mindful of how certain decisions will play out and how online mobs might amplify them.

It is helpful to also put morals and ethics into a system such as a company. Let's look at Artificial Intelligence (AI) which is usually in the news these days. Google was recently hit with a complaint that they aren't diverse enough and don't treat AI rollouts with enough care. I can't speak to these specific arguments, but I can provide my thoughts on AI ethics. It seems the future is making us revisit the past.

Every good system will always have checks and balances. Take US politics, for example. It's common to hear that "US politics is broken" and that "democracy is dying." While I can't predict the future, I can see that the US political system's design has beautiful checks and balances. Congress checks the Senate and vice versa. Both houses check the power of the president. The president himself can check over ambitious legal actions by providing federal pardons to whoever they please.

It's easy to disagree with any of these specific parts of the system. We may think that the Senate is blocking laws from being enacted or may complain that the president has too much power, especially when it comes to pardons. However, we can't look at the system individually; we have to look at it holistically. Ethics and morality are one of the lenses through which we can analyze systems.

The same applies to AI. We can't simply focus on the code and the models. We need to look at the entire system. How will this AI program affect our customers? What is the legal liability? What are the moral implications of the decisions the model is making? I don't think you can just let "facts speak for themselves." Our most important institutions don't function this way. Take the example of Facebook, which is getting pressure from all sides for their content moderation policies.

They recently implemented a committee board that will look at specific decisions, such as banning a specific user, and determining if that decision was correct. The board has the power to overturn the decision. This is an excellent example of a check in the system. Systems and companies need checks and balances. We can implement them as policies or as part of our culture. These checks and balances can help deal with some of the trickiest positions that we will come across. You may not outright ban politics at work, but your culture has a strong teamwork value even with those you might not like.

AI is seen as a technology of absolutes, but it is being deployed in a world of grays. The world isn't black and white. Some of the most important institutions like politics and law were designed to deal with the ambiguity, and AI will have to be the same. Companies should understand the ethics of AI decisions, which means understanding the past, as humanity has been debating ethics and morals for a long time.

In the following pages, we will look at situations that have challenged our ideas of morality and how we reconcile opposing views. These decisions are callous, and no amount of data can help. You need to look deep into what we value as individuals and as teams. It's from that vantage point that we can then make these highly charged decisions. I hope that you can avoid an internal blowout as the one Basecamp suffered.

BEHIND THE DECISION: NETFLIX AND THEIR CULTURE OF FEAR

In 2018, the *Wall Street Journal* wrote about Netflix's "Culture of Fear."[*] The 4,500-word piece talked about executive firings and Netflix's radical transparency ethos. Netflix takes its culture seriously, and much has been written about it. It all started when they released a 124-slide deck detailing the principles or ideas on which their culture was built. The document went viral. Sheryl Sandberg, COO at Facebook, called it "one of the most important documents ever to come out of Silicon Valley." Did Netflix create an innovative culture, or did their employees live in fear?

Reed Hastings, CEO, and Founder of Netflix, actually released a book diving deeper into their culture. Titled *No Rules Rules*, Mr. Hastings' book shares the lessons that have helped Netflix thrive. He is joined by Erin Meyer, an expert in organizational culture. The book details the key turning points in the company's history and how each of those decisions led to an important pillar. Netflix has a unique culture. It was bound to attract negative attention.

Let's start with the facts. Netflix believes that their company is like a sports team and not a family. As long as you can contribute to the team, then you're in. The moment you can no longer do that, you're out. We see this all the time in actual sports teams. Players get traded without any warning. You could be getting ready to play a game when the news comes down, and you'd have to pack up your things and move to another city. Sports teams rarely keep players for sentimental reasons, and everyone involved accepts this as "just business."

Netflix has done the same thing. They have let go of executives who were instrumental in helping them establish their DVD businesses after transitioning to digital content. They have let go of great people in the early stages who couldn't see themselves as part of a public company. Employees are told of these facts when they join the company. In exchange for this high-pressure environment, Netflix consistently pays top of the market in all of its positions. Working

---

[*] "At Netflix, Radical Transparency and Blunt Firings Unsettle the Ranks," *Wall Street Journal*, accessed April 15, 2021, https://www.wsj.com/articles/at-netflix-radical-transparency-and-blunt-firings-unsettle-the-ranks-1540497174

at Netflix means that you will be one of the highest earners in your field. You can even negotiate higher salaries in any given year if you have evidence to support your case. Netflix doesn't limit you to arbitrarily salary raises like 2% "cost of living" increases.

Netflix has also embraced radical honesty or candor. The examples given in the book are extreme. If you're fumbling a presentation, people from the audience will tell you what you're doing wrong. If you made a mistake, someone will talk to you about it and ask what happened. If someone disagrees with your idea, it is disloyal not to share your thoughts. You're expected to be honest with everyone, including the CEO. You could email him with honest feedback and expect him to read it and consider it. Feedback isn't handed out randomly. Employees are trained on how to properly give feedback.

The organization also lives the values of transparency by making all numbers available to everyone. You could easily see the latest numbers in subscribers, revenue, profit, etc. Netflix is a public company, so this may sound like a crazy idea. However, employees can actually see all the numbers at any given time. In fact, an employee could see the numbers right before they are released to Wall Street, making it easy to commit fraud through inside trading. The company understands the risks and communicates that to all employees. Honesty comes with power, and every employee has to make the right choices.

The high salaries, high freedom, and high expectations lead to what some people may call fear. If you join Netflix, you're expected to perform at a high level. You're entrusted with a large amount of freedom to make your decisions and drive success. However, you're also walking on a tightrope. Mistakes can be amplified as the scale increases. A million-dollar content deal might go through different levels of approvals in other companies, each buffering the previous one. At Netflix, one person will sign that deal. That's the person who is supposed to be closest to the decision and has the best perspective on the merits of the deal.

Netflix's culture has clearly worked. They have survived the transition away from DVDs into a streaming world. They also thrived by becoming their own content studio instead of constantly dealing with tougher requirements from content providers. The company was worth over $200 billion dollars at the time of this writing. The future looks tough. Every content company is setting up its own streaming platform and locking away its content. I would bet that Netflix will continue to put out amazing content. Their culture of high performance will have a huge role in that. Their decisions to embrace freedom have proven effective.

DOING WHAT'S RIGHT EVEN WHEN IT ISN'T POPULAR OR EASY

In the 1970s, a group of students was being pulled to Chicago like a magnet.* They were all there for the same reason: to study economics under Milton Friedman and Arnold Harborage. The students came from Latin America and other countries, and the deal was simple. You would get scholarships to study at the University of Chicago, but you would then have to go back to your home country and share the learned ideas. These students were picking up modern economic ideas around free markets and incentives. Many of them went back home and tried to implement these ideas.

As you can imagine, they had a tough time getting their ideas into government. They were academics with little or no political connections. Dictators ran Latin American countries, and the corruption level was incredibly high. The fear of communism—which Fidel Castro in Cuba magnified in the 1950s—meant that countries like America would rather support a dictator than let the country fall into communism. This was the case with Chile, which was ruled by Augusto Pinochet. To say that Pinochet was brutal would be an understatement. He managed the country with an iron fist and would become one of the most notorious dictators of the era. Somehow, Pinochet's government got its hands on the ideas from the students from Chicago—nicknamed the Chicago Boys.

Pinochet agreed to let them implement their ideas while he still maintained political control over the country. The reforms started in 1975, and the results were amazing. If we look at Chile today, we would see a country that quadrupled its income per capita and became the most prosperous country in the region. Chile improved across many of the metrics that matter to us as a society: maternal mortality, proper sanitation, education, and others. It currently ranks 44th in the UN's

---

* "The Boys Who Got to Remake an Economy," Slate, accessed April 19, 2021, https://slate.com/business/2016/01/in-chicago-boys-the-story-of-chilean-economists-who-studied-in-america-and-then-remade-their-country.html

Human Development Index, and it has the highest levels of overall freedom and civil and personal liberties. The reforms under Pinochet worked.

Not everything is perfect in Chile. There's still inequality—as in most countries—and the country is currently undergoing a rewrite of its constitution. It's unclear what is driving the dissatisfaction among the Chilean people. The country does much better than its peers, but there's deeply rooted unfairness in some institutions. The worry for some is that Chile will get overtaken by a populist reform that can derail or erase Chile's gains in the past 35 years. The future of Chile is uncertain, and it will be interesting to see how it develops.

Young Chileans today feel conflicted about their past. While Pinochet was killing people left and right, the Chicago Boys were implementing their ideas. These ideas led to the Chile we see today. It felt like a deal with the devil, and young Chileans aren't sure if it was worth it. They have pushed for the largest constitutional change since Pinochet. Perhaps there's an attempt to erase the past or to move on from it. Older Chileans who lived through the Pinochet regime felt like a sacrifice that has proven to be worth it. It was the right decision for the present. Leaders are faced with these kinds of decisions all the time. How do you do what's right even when it isn't popular or easy?

Frameworks and other decision-making ideas are helpful, but they need a critical ingredient: courage. I see it all the time when working with clients. They know what the right decision is, but they lack enough courage to make it. As a leader, you want to know when a decision requires more information and when it simply requires more courage. Letting go of employees is one of those decisions that usually boils down to courage. You know that this person isn't performing and that this job isn't a right fit for them; the missing piece is the courage to let them go.

Saying that Margaret Thatcher was a controversial Prime Minister would be an understatement. She guided Britain through one of its toughest post-war periods and made consistent tough choices. She famously said that "we will stand on principle or we will not stand at all." Courage seemed to be in excess supply in her world.

Margaret Thatcher focused on her principles and what she thought was right for the country. She didn't let the protests or even a bombing attempt derail her. She stuck by her principles and made her decisions. Not all of them were right, but she moved in a direction. The moving aspect of decisions is quite important. It's easier to redirect energy once it is in motion than when it is standing still. Thinking about trying to turn a car with no momentum versus while driving.

Decision-making models don't usually talk about courage. They assume that once you have all the facts, you will make the right decision. It's just a matter of going through a checklist and arriving at the final answer. In other words, making decisions is like math. You might have different ways of calculating a result, but the answer is always the same.

I think this misses a huge portion of how decisions are actually made. Margaret Thatcher talked about how different philosophies shaped Britain and the United States. Britain (and Europe to an extent) were shaped by their history, while their philosophy shaped America. Europe was constrained to what was possible based on what happened to them, but Americans thought of what could be. Manifest destiny permeated all of American society.

In companies, we would call this culture. The culture shapes how decisions are made. Do you operate in a culture of fear when it comes to mistakes? Is your culture able to support failures? The more your culture allows for missteps, the less courage you need. The opposite is true. You need even more courage if your company's culture frowns upon making the wrong bets. No checklist or framework can override bad culture.

Courage is also only rewarded in hindsight. We know we need courage but don't expect to get instant gratification from it. Making the right decision might take months or years before it shows that you took the right step. Your courage may be unrewarded except in your own mind. You need your own metrics and principles for judging the usage of your courage. Hindsight may prove you right, but it will take time.

The natural next question is: how do you build more courage? I don't think it entails going into the jungle and trying to live off the land. You also don't need to relocate to a monastery and engage in Rocky-style training montages. Instead, you can build more courage by rethinking how you approach your everyday decisions. Beliefs often come up in self-help circles, but it is a useful concept for our discussion. In particular, I think you should work on adopting three new beliefs that will influence all of your decisions, including your toughest ones.

Belief One: Know You Can Adjust

One of the major roadblocks in tough decisions is the sense that we are dealing with finality. If we make the wrong choice, we will be stuck. Our minds tend to catastrophize, so the perception of being stuck has been magnified. Choosing the wrong goal to hit in strategy will lead to massive layoffs, bankruptcy, and who knows what else. We sometimes see some decisions as subway trains. Once you get on it, there's no stopping or changing course.

In reality, we don't actually deal with these kinds of decisions often. We talked about permanence in another chapter to check that you can understand how easily malleable any given decision might be. In this section, I want to discuss adopting a mindset of "I can figure it out." If we choose the wrong objective in our strategic planning, we will adjust and find the right one. If I run into an issue at work, I can find the solution or find the person that knows it. There are always options.

Adopting this mindset means that we don't have to fret over wrong decisions. We can do our best, weigh the options, and think about obstacles. If we miss something that never crossed our minds, we can figure it out. Organizations have been working on shifting into agile teams that fundamentally work off this idea. There's only so much you can analyze or think about before making a decision, so agility and flexibility are more important.

Think about it as Google Maps. Many of us now use GPS to guide us to our destination. It's so common that we don't even know the structure of the streets anymore. Without a GPS, we couldn't easily get to certain locations. GPS is great and perfect for most situations. However, we also need to be comfortable without it. If we run into traffic that the software didn't know about, we want to take a right and find a way around it. We know our final destination, and we will change our course depending on what we see in front of us. We can figure it out even without technology.

Belief Two: Be Vulnerable

Vulnerability has become one of the most popular words in the world of psychology. Younger generations are growing with the idea that it's ok to share their feelings and concerns. Talk therapy is widely accepted. It's not always easy to be vulnerable, especially in the common dynamics of a company. A leader is supposed to be strong, right? Being vulnerable might mean that you aren't strong or, worst of all, that you don't know what you're doing.

Homer said that courage "is when you sacrifice your own well-being for the sake of the survival of a layer higher than yours." He never talked about being strong or having all the answers. Being open with your team and colleagues can take the weight from the world off your shoulders. I understand that not every topic can be easily discussed with your team. In those situations, consider finding peer groups where you can get comfortable and share tricky challenges. Just don't hold it in because of some external expectation.

They say it is lonely at the top, and I think that is particularly true for executives. You're now in this position where you're supposed to have the answers, but that's impossible. What you need is a culture where people can talk about mistakes openly—including you—and you need peers that can support you. You'll realize that challenges aren't unique to you, and other people have insights that could prove incredibly valuable.

Belief Three: Treat People like Adults

The third belief to adopt is how you treat other adults. In essence, treat them as grown individuals who are capable of making their own decisions. We sometimes worry about how a decision might impact someone. If we fire an employee, will they be able to take the news, or will they fall into depression from which they will never escape? We need to give people more credit. Humans are incredibly resilient when put under pressure. We may be doing more harm than good by not letting someone go or sharing negative feedback.

If we treat people as healthy and mature adults, then certain conversations and actions can take place. Don't assume that your preferences are what other people want. If someone shows you that they haven't maturely handled things, you may need to shift your approach. Don't make that your default. Lying is mentally taxing. You have to maintain two stories in your mind: the truth and the lie. Focus on reducing the "white lies" from your life.

A couple of years ago, I visited Oahu, Hawaii. It's a beautiful island with amazing beaches. We went to the north of the island where surfing takes place. During surfing season, the waves here are huge. A height of 10–15 feet is common. Surfers love these big waves. In the Inner Game of Tennis, Tim Gallwey talks about the rush of tackling big waves. He says that "only against the big waves that he is required to use all his skill, all his courage and concentration to overcome; only then can he realize the true limits of his capacities."

Decisions that require courage are similar to big waves. Those are the best opportunities for you to use all your skills and concentration. Smaller decisions are important, but big decisions are where people really shine. We shouldn't fear these decisions but look forward to them. Regardless of the outcome, we will learn something. We will build courage. We will be better for future decisions.

BEHIND THE DECISION: RENAISSANCE POPES

There are six men who profoundly shaped our world with their decisions—or perhaps their lack of a decision. The six men seemed unprepared for their jobs and ended up accelerating a revolution that can still be felt today. The six men were the Renaissance Popes whose corruption and incompetence have become legendary. To understand who they were, we have to first understand the world in which they grew up.

The Renaissance Papacy period took place between 1470 and 1530. There were actually eight popes during this period, but two of them were only in power for a few days and are usually excluded from this period. Trust me, those two popes are lucky to be ignored and not be grouped with the other six. Over 60 years, the papacy would elect questionable representatives that would make terrible decisions.

The six men who came to power were products of their time. This was the era of extravagance by families like the Medici. Rich families competed to build their wealth and show it to the world. They would consistently hire the best artists and sculptors and ask them to build things in their name. Money was no object. They were also constantly engaged in wars. The states of Italy weren't a unified country yet, and they were always jockeying for power.

One of the ways to gain power was to join the Catholic Church. You could become a Cardinal or take other positions without actually being a priest. Everyone was religious at the time, so it's not like people who didn't believe in God joined the Church. However, they weren't joining in spreading the message; they were joining to further their own personal interests. The Catholic Church was meant to symbolize God on Earth, but some of its officials simply wanted wealth and power.

The six popes—Sixtus IV, Innocent VIII, Alexander VI, Julius II, Leo X, and Clement VII—were no different. Leo X was actually a Medici, and his father had groomed him to become a pope from an early age. He held high-ranking positions within the church when he was just a teenager. These positions were earned by simply paying for them, which was a common practice at the time.

The election of these men and the decisions they made weren't based on what was best for the Church. They brought their extravagant lifestyles into the Church and spent money like there was no tomorrow. People noticed the corruption, and they were asking for reforms. They wanted the Church to become what it was meant to be by Peter and Paul. The six popes, however, rejected reforms and assumed that someone else would do them. The lack of decision is what is interesting to us in this book.

Barbara W. Tuchman, the author of *The March of Folly*, talks about how these six men engaged in folly strategies. They knew that by not seriously considering reforms, something was bound to happen to the Church. They acted against the best interests of their institutions and contributed to what would happen in the early 15th century. Their advisors told them to engage in reforms and call a council—the common way for new policies to be developed and adopted by the church.

None of the six men did what they were supposed to. They all died without engaging in reforms. In 1517, Martin Luther would write his famous *Ninety-Five Theses* and start the reformation. It would forever split the Church into what we see today. Protestant religions were born out of the reformation, and the Church lost the power to influence them.

The six popes feared what reforms might do to them personally. They overestimated the power of the Church and failed to properly weigh all the variables of their decisions. In effect, they created a bubble that filtered out what was going on outside of Rome. Their lack of decisions opened the door for the Reformation, which changed how we view and engage with religion today. Sometimes, decisions can have repercussions over thousands of years. The six Renaissance Popes were not ready for that responsibility.

THE FUTURE OF LEADERSHIP AND HOW TO PREPARE

It's fascinating to see how leadership has expanded over time. Hundreds of years ago, we would have likely only considered army generals and kings to be leaders. They had to literally lead men into war or manage an entire kingdom. Today, we hear leadership be applied to any situation. Star athletes are questioned for their "leadership capabilities." Managers at all levels are taught how to be better leaders. We even talk about "community leaders."

John Gardner said that leadership is the "process of persuasion or example by which an individual induces a group to pursue objectives." We now expect that everyone can take up leadership positions. You might even be a leader for your family. It's not about how many people you manage or the impact of the group but about helping others. Leadership has permeated into society beyond the governments and military. We actively discuss how to build better leaders among our children. We want to have more people take up the calling of helping others even if they engage in national politics or lead armies into war.

Naturally, we should then think about the future of leadership. What things should young leaders or people who are aspiring to be leaders should work on? What skills should they build, and what skills are outdated? Who should they learn from? These are the questions that are being debated within companies, universities, and even at home. I don't have all the answers but let me give you five ideas that every future leader should know.

Leadership Is Not Status, Power, or Authority

The idea of a leader deciding the fate of millions of people is going away. Understand me, those types of leaders still exist and will continue to exist. However, leadership isn't about status, power, or authority. I'm sure you can imagine someone who has any of these attributes (or perhaps all three) but isn't a leader. People wouldn't follow them to the grocery store, let alone through tumultuous times.

Instead, leadership is about showing others in what direction you should head. You might not know the exact solution or path to success, but a leader is confident in their ability to deal with ambiguity, challenges, and roadblocks. They can tell people to follow them as they go into a dark cave without a map or a light. Working as a team, they can find the exit out of the cave.

Becoming a leader might naturally bring you status, power, or authority. Don't confuse them with the essence of leadership—helping others—and be skeptical of them. Any of the three can corrupt even the best leaders.

We see it in someone like Robert Moses, who single-handedly built New York's parks and highways but was eventually changed by the power that came from it. If you seek them, you might find them, but you won't be a leader.

Faster Decisions in a Complex World

We all feel that our world is getting faster. Part of that is driven by technology and having instant access to almost everything. It's wild to me how our perceptions (including mine) can shift so quickly. A package that takes weeks to arrive at your house is seen as incredibly slow. Why can't it be delivered in days or, better yet, tomorrow? Decisions are following the same trend. As a leader, you don't have months or years to think about things. You need to make the right decisions in days, hours, or minutes.

Leaders need to equip themselves with the right tools for the job. A typewriter is a fine machine, but it is not suited for our digital world. Using a typewriter instead of a laptop would be foolish. The same applies to your decision-making models. Don't use models that were designed in a world where time was always available. Upgrade your models for the 21st century.

Adopting Styles to Younger Generations

Every generation changes expectations based on the conditions they grew up in. Leaders need to adjust to the younger generations. It used to be that young people had to mold themselves to whatever style their boss had. If their boss was aggressive and critical, that was just life. You can't expect your boss to adjust to your preferences. That's not how the world works.

We see a massive change in the other direction. Companies and leaders are being forced to adapt to the younger generations. You can't just say anything you want and expect your employees to accept it. Leaders are being asked to make decisions while thinking about politics, social issues, and the environment. Cultures are being adapted to the kind of feedback and environment that suits the younger generation.

I'm not saying that these changes are good or bad. I'm saying that they are happening and that leaders need to adjust. I do think that there's an aspect of going too far. Cancel culture and the general fear of saying the wrong things are extreme examples of this shift. Nonetheless, we can't shape our outside culture, we can simply respond to it. That's what future leaders will need to continue to do.

Transparency

Expecting a leader to be vulnerable used to be a crazy idea. That idea is still true in some places, but we are seeing more leaders embrace transparency and honesty. They share what they are thinking and the unknowns of the situation. People are also changing their expectations. They don't expect leaders to have all the answers. They simply want them to be willing to work through the issues and be open to feedback.

As a leader, you need to find the balance between being transparent and coming across as clueless. You do it by recognizing the appropriate channels for sharing. Some decisions could be easily shared with your team members, while others should only be shared with peers. You will also need to gauge or test how much transparency is needed in different situations.

Knowing Your Medium

In 1964, Marshall McLuhan coined the phrase "The medium is the message." He referred to how the medium (TV, print, etc.) affected how the content of a message was conveyed. Today, the phrase couldn't be any more true. We come across clips on social media that seemed to tell a story until we see the entire video. Or we hear about remarks that someone made that turned out to be completely different once put into context.

Leaders need to be highly aware of the medium in which they are communicating. Digital channels—even channels like video—aren't the same as in-person. Chat tools like Slack make it even harder to fully communicate emotions and intentions. Future leaders will need to have a good grasp of using the different mediums available to them. They will need to select the best one and not the easiest. Calling someone might be harder than an email, but it might be the right choice.

Future leaders will stumble in the same way past ones have. Some things are so new that consequences might not be that clear. We saw bosses who wanted to show appreciation to their employees while working from home so much that they decided to visit them at their homes while video streaming it to the rest of the company. You could see how employees might feel annoyed by their boss coming to their house unannounced while the entire company watches. The intention was good, but the execution was not. That was not the proper medium.

Leaders will learn from all these examples, and they will set new rules for engagement. I think the future of leadership is bright. It is now a topic being actively discussed and studied, not just for the select few but also for everyone. Making the right decisions will be an essential component of good leadership, and I hope this book gives you the necessary tools for your journey.

CHAPTER SUMMARY

- Good decision-making is even more important for leaders, as we can see from public examples like Basecamp.
- The LDMM (Leadership Decision-Making Matrix) provides you with three options for involving your team.
- Think about morality within the context of your life and company. It is not a vague concept but one that has serious implications.
- You can adjust to any situation if you have the right beliefs.
- Leadership is not status, power, or authority—instead, it's about helping others.

8

The 7 Pillars of Effective Decision-Making for Individuals and Teams

If you walk through the streets of downtown Vancouver, all you can hear are the sounds of construction: trucks beeping as they back up, hammers smashing into hard metal, people shuffling material, and automated machinery putting things together. Vancouver is going through a construction boom as I write this in early 2021. It's not limited to just the downtown core. Buildings are going up all over the city at an accelerated pace.

The boom isn't a surprise. Vancouver, Canada, is consistently listed as one of the most expensive cities for buying real estate. Housing is one of the major issues in the city and one that no one seems to know how to fix. Despite the high prices, condos and houses are selling like there's no tomorrow. It is common to see listings sell for thousands of dollars over the asking price, without subjects and within days of being listed. It's a good time to be a selling real estate agent in Vancouver!

I have been watching a building be constructed right in front of my apartment. Every day, I see more pieces added to the facade and the foundations. I'm always amazed to see buildings come together from nothing. You first see the foundational pillars, see the floors, and see external things like windows. Once all that is done, I imagine they add the internal components: plumbing, electricity, and eventually, amenities like stoves and dishwashers.

In developed countries, it is rare to see a building collapse on its own. We have stringent building codes that establish how buildings should be contracted to handle the weather and day-to-day pressures.

DOI: 10.4324/9781003185383-8

We know how to make sure that the pillars can withstand whatever is thrown at them. Building codes even try to imagine what it might feel like to be hit by an earthquake—which Vancouver has been expecting for years. Decisions also have building codes or pillars that underpin them.

I have identified seven pillars that tend to be part of almost every decision. These pillars will be present in any of the three strategies that we have covered so far, and it is important to understand them. We can't build on shoddy foundations like buildings can't shoot up toward the sky on weak pillars. The seven pillars are speed, permanence, ownership, loops, fundamentals, self-interest, and the future. You'll learn how each of these pillars affects your decisions and how to make sure they are sturdy and reliable (Figure 8.1).

The pillars apply to your personal and professional decisions. Speed, for example, is the pillar that affects how quickly you make a decision. It's important to make the right decision, but it's just as vital to make a decision rapidly. Opportunities have windows that will eventually close. A good quarterback is looking for the best person to throw the ball at, but he needs to do it quickly before getting pummeled into the ground. Each of the pillars will flesh out the three strategies you have learned thus far and help you level them up further.

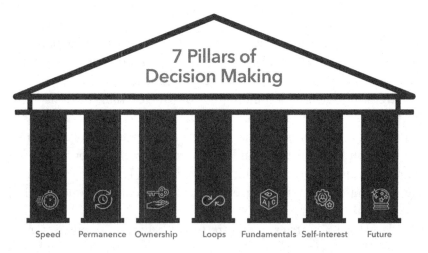

FIGURE 8.1
7 Pillars of decision-making.

BEHIND THE DECISION: THE SEARCH FOR LOST MEANING

Poggio Bracciolini was a man of many talents. His handwriting was beautiful, he spoke perfect Latin, and served as the secretary for many Popes. He was, in the most literal sense, the guardian of secrets for the Vatican. He served seven Popes in 50 years and was present through many pivotal moments for the Catholic Church. He spent most of his adult life in papal service, but he had other passions. Passions that would eventually change the world.

In 1415, the church went through upheaval when John XXIII—labeled the Antipope for opposing the person who was eventually recognized as the true successor to Saint Peter—was deposed by the Council of Constance. The inner turmoil gave Poggio two years of leisure time in 1416 and 1417, respectively. He used this time in one of these other passions: manuscript hunting.

Poggio was part of a group of people who called themselves "humanists." They loved to study from the oldest books, those written by Plato, Socrates, and others who came before them. The trouble was that many of these books had been lost to fires and other natural causes. If any of these books existed, they likely resided in one place: monasteries.

Monasteries took the duty of teaching monks how to read and write seriously. They undertook this task with efficiency and passion. They maintain large libraries containing all kinds of books. Being able to preserve these books through centuries wasn't an easy task. After multiple uses, books would eventually start to fall apart. This meant that the monks had to copy the books constantly to avoid losing the knowledge of fate.

Monasteries were also influenced by the changing times. As Christianity took hold in the world, books by non-Christians weren't seen as appropriate. Scholars like Plato and Socrates worshipped multiple gods, which was ludicrous by that point. How could anyone bear to read their works on philosophy and mathematics? This kind of thinking led the monks to overwrite their original works with more suitable ideas for their time. For example, Archimedes's work on calculus was almost lost through this rewriting process until someone discovered the remains of these ideas.

Poggio and other humanists knew that monks were sitting on a goldmine of knowledge. They just had to find a way into the monasteries and then get permission to examine their books. In one of these journeys, Poggio discovered his most famous find: *De Rerum Natura* by Lucretius. The title translates to "On the Nature of Things," and Poggio spotted it in 1417 because he remembered reading a mention of it by Cicero. The book is a Latin poem of 7,400 lines, divided into six books, giving a unique world description.

The book took years to be copied over and shared by other humanists. The ideas inside the book would eventually influence the Renaissance, the Reformation, the founding fathers of the United States, and others. The poem was written sometime between 99 BC and 55 BC and had breakthrough ideas, including atomism (the world is made up of tiny atoms), the role of chance, and a world that evolved randomly instead of being guided by a divine hand. At that time, these ideas were controversial and crazy. In today's world, we call these ideas modern science.

The decision to seek out these manuscripts by Poggio and others like him saved knowledge from being lost forever. The decision to save this specific book, *De Rerum Natura*, would later influence the modern world. We never know how these decisions may come together in the future, but sometimes they play out in spectacular ways.

7 PILLARS FOR EFFECTIVE DECISION-MAKING

Each of the following pillars will provide you with a new clue on how you make decisions. As you read through them, keep in mind a few decisions that worked out quite well and a few where things didn't go as expected. You can contrast these two categories through the lens of each of the pillars. If a building is missing a pillar, it doesn't mean that it will collapse. However, missing too many pillars will weaken the entire foundation.

Speed

Speed is paramount to making decisions. This idea can be counterintuitive because we can all think of situations where someone (or ourselves) made decisions too quickly. We rushed to a conclusion and regretted our actions.

Speed can backfire, but there's also the possibility of moving too slow. I was working with a client during the height of the COVID-19 pandemic, and it became clear that the uncertainty paralyzed them.

Our project revolved around better visualizing their data, but they kept delaying the launch. After enough delays, I realized that they weren't comfortable making this decision, and I wasn't able to get through to them. If they had launched faster, we would have learned new things and adjusted our course. A ship doesn't wait until all the stars, weather, and winds align in its favor. You set the course and make adjustments as needed.

Executives get paid to get results that come from making high-quality decisions. They also need to make decisions quickly and with little information. I'm always surprised when I see a team debating a course of action for months. They aren't learning anything new, but there's a fear that prevents them from pulling the trigger. I think it comes down to a lack of trust in being able to fix any mistakes. If you make a decision and you're wrong, then you're done—no second chances.

I admit that there are some areas in life where you literally won't get second chances, but those are the exceptions that prove the rule. Take something like cancer treatment. Doctors will analyze your symptoms, run tests, and then make a diagnosis. Based on your condition, they may recommend an option like chemotherapy. If that doesn't work as expected, then the doctor will try a different treatment. Doctors do their best, but they aren't fortune tellers. They have to get moving before they know what is working and what isn't.

Luckily for most of us, we aren't dealing with life or death. Instead, we deal with problems that aren't permanent or final. Churchill once said that "success is not final, failure is not fatal: it is the courage to continue that counts." Have the courage to make decisions rapidly but deliberately. Run them through a process where you weigh the pros and cons but don't get stuck in analysis paralysis. At some point, the best decision is to move forward.

Permanence

We can't talk about speed without diving into permanence. Some decisions are impermanent. Where you decide to hang a picture frame is quite flexible. It will take you a few minutes to change it to a different location.

Who you marry is a more permanent decision, but you still have options for change. A decision can have three types of permanence: high, medium, or low. Each one requires a slightly different approach, and it's important not to assume that the permanence is higher than it really is (Figure 8.2).

High permanent decisions are some of the most tricky and important decisions that we might make. I think they are rare in our lives, but we still come across them. Choosing to have kids, life-threatening medical procedures, and committing a crime are examples of high permanent decisions. These decisions will have a lasting impact on our lives, and we can't easily just "walk" away from them. As you think of examples from your own life, you will realize that they aren't that common unless you're a brain surgeon—then, in that case, you might be making these kinds of decisions every day.

Medium permanent decisions will impact our lives for months or even years, but eventually, we will be able to move on. Buying a house, moving cities for a new job, and getting married are examples of medium permanent decisions. The length of permanency is different for everybody, and there is room for debate. You could buy a house and then sell it a few weeks later, albeit at a financial cost.

Medium permanent decisions are perhaps the most difficult to deal with because we tend to invest in them, making it harder for us to walk away from there. The psychological bias of "sunken cost"—the idea that you already invested money or time so that it alone makes it worthwhile to continue on a path—is prevalent with these decisions. They are also common enough that we will deal with them regularly.

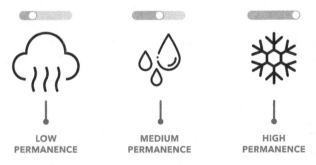

Stickiness of Decisions

| LOW PERMANENCE | MEDIUM PERMANENCE | HIGH PERMANENCE |

FIGURE 8.2
Stickiness of decisions.

Low permanent decisions are the easiest to deal with, even though we come across them every day. Choosing what to eat for lunch, what driving route to take home, and how to spend our evenings are all examples of low permanent decisions. These decisions have a minimal impact on our lives—typically measured in minutes or hours—and are easily reversible. We can still get stuck on these decisions, but it's more of a mental issue than a real one.

As permanence goes up, your decision-making process has to be stricter. Choosing to elope to Vegas with a person you just met can have disastrous consequences. You would be creating a high permanent decision as if it were a low permanent one. There are two challenges to be aware of here. The first is properly assigning permanence to each decision. The second is ensuring that you're able to spend the appropriate amount of time with each type of permanence. The decision-making frameworks we have covered would expand or shrink depending on the permanence.

Ownership

Ownership is the ability to take responsibility for the right decisions. Think of ownership as a spectrum. On one end, you have taken too much responsibility for too many decisions. This is the person that makes everyone's problem their own. They can end up feeling overwhelmed and frustrated because they took ownership of decisions that aren't truly theirs, to begin with. On the other end, you can take too little responsibility for your decisions. This is the person where nothing is their fault, or negative things just happen to them.

In a work environment, you can have an executive or leader who takes ownership of all the decisions. This is the micromanager who has to get involved in every decision, no matter how small. Everything has to be approved by them, as if they have some kind of magic power over the outcomes of decisions. You can also have individuals who don't take enough responsibility for relevant decisions.

The lack of ownership is usually coupled with an executive or manager who takes too much ownership. I constantly meet executives who tell me that they are exhausted at making all the decisions for their team. They don't want to micromanage anyone, but they are forced into the role. We'll talk more about getting your team to make their own decisions, but be aware of this relationship. I sometimes meet micromanagers who admit that they are too involved, but they don't actually want to change. They enjoy the current setup for multiple reasons—ego, satisfaction, control, power, etc.—and you can't help someone who doesn't want to be helped.

We also need to think about the level of involvement that we are asking of others in decisions. Nassim Taleb wrote about having "skin the game" and how this is essential for any system to function. When politicians argue for war, they typically aren't the ones to actually do the fighting. The lack of "skin in the game" can disrupt these decisions. Mr. Taleb argues that people make drastically different decisions when they are affected by the outcomes.

You can see this at play in your personal life, but you should also consider adding more "skin in the game" within your teams. Working with individuals to ensure that their performance is tied to compensation—while also ensuring that they have the freedom to affect it—is the key to adding ownership to decisions. Westjet, the airline, has built its culture on the idea that every employee should act like an owner. It isn't merely empty words. Westjet has a profit-sharing plan and other incentives to encourage this behavior.

Loops

Some decisions happen all the time. You may not know this the first time you face one of these decisions, but you will definitely know it by the third or fourth time. Decision loops are perfect opportunities to delegate and to systemize. In business, think of all the decisions that your employees will face regularly. These are all places where you could help them use frameworks to make their own decisions.

A couple of years ago, I was staying at the Hilton hotel in Miami Beach. I had a long flight coming from the West Coast, and all I wanted was to check into my room and relax. After a few minutes, I found myself walking into my room. I put all my bags down and started to look for the light switch. My room was dark, and I could barely see anything. I couldn't find this switch for the life of me and started to think that this is just how the room was designed.

I suddenly got an SMS from the Hilton front desk asking if I had any questions about the room. As it turns out, I did! I texted back, asking about the light switch. They replied that the only lights were those that I could already see. The reply wasn't constructive. I then happened to stumble upon the switch which showered the room with light. The switch wasn't hidden, but I simply missed it due to my tiredness.

I think the SMS was a fantastic idea from Hilton, but the execution wasn't great. The front desk could have called or sent someone over to help with my question. They had already started the effort but dropped the ball five yards from the touchdown. Someone at Hilton recognized this as a decision loop. Guests check-in, and they might have questions, so let's send them an automated SMS to see if we can help. That was a great decision, but I think they need to empower their front desk staff to make judgment calls to deal with questions.

In your work and life, think of all the decisions that you face often. Loops tie very well into the Turtleneck Principle. Instead of deciding every day you will go to the gym, simply make a choice and then stick to it. You can always adjust to changing circumstances, but your original decision will be fine most of the time. Within your team, loops should be like warning hazard lights on a dark road. If you find yourself making the same decisions repeatedly, that is a clear sign that you could be delegating the decision to someone else.

I work with a marketing team that is struggling to make their own choices. The executive team constantly micromanaged them. It was no surprise that the marketing team had lost the energy to tackle even simple decisions like choosing what campaigns to run. The company had to work on letting people make their own decisions, especially recurring ones. The executive realized that by making micromanaging a decision in the present, they were harming the future. Letting go of the reins didn't happen overnight, but it started with decision loops.

Fundamentals

Occasionally, you will encounter decisions that are heavily influenced by changing fundamental conditions. Many of these decisions (or opportunities) tend to manifest in some kind of innovation. For example, take the stock market. Fifty years ago, it used to cost upwards of $100 to buy a stock. This was the transaction fee that made the buying possible, not the actual stock price. Your stockbroker had to call a guy who called another guy who then bought the stock for you. Everyone involved had to get paid, and that was the transaction fee.

Over time, the transaction fee started to drop. Improvements in technology such as computers made it possible to complete these transactions without as much human involvement. Eventually, everything was automated and the transaction fee of purchasing stocks became $0. At this point in the story, Robinhood appears. They offer zero-fee stock trading because the fundamental conditions have changed dramatically. If you were analyzing a decision related to the stock market, you would need to consider these fundamental changes.

In our personal lives, we encounter similar changes as we get older. When you're in your twenties, your body might feel invincible. You can stay up all night and make it into work by 8 am, ready to tackle another day. You barely miss a beat, and you could do these kinds of nights back to back. As you get older, even missing a couple of hours of sleep can throw you off completely. If you're considering a new health or fitness routine, you need to consider how your body is changing and how to best respond. You can't base your plan on what you could do ten years ago.

In your life, you need to recognize the fundamentals and how they might be changing. The changes may be fast or slow, but there needs to be an acceptance of them. We all hear about situations when someone is holding on to the past and refusing to "move on." In your personal life, ignoring fundamentals will be frustrating. It can be disastrous to launch a product to a customer segment that no longer exists at work.

Self-Interest

There's a lot of things that we do for our own self-interest. What we eat, what we wear, how we spend our time, and many other things are sometimes just catering to our self-interest. I spoke about self-interest in the chapter on emotions—under Personal. Self-interest is so important that it was worth mentioning twice. In this section, I want to talk about short- vs long-term self-interest.

Choosing to eat that slice of cake demonstrates the conflict. In the short term, our self-interest would be greatly benefited by eating the cake. It's going to be delicious and worth every bite. If you don't know, I'm a huge dessert person. A part of me is completely rooting for my imaginary example person to eat the cake. In the long term, eating the cake might go against your health plans. Perhaps you're trying to lose weight, or your blood sugar is too high. How do you balance the short- and long-term self-interest?

It's not easy. The example above is one of the most difficult issues with any health regimen. As you think about your and other self-interest, you will need to determine if you want to fulfill the short- or long-term version. You might make a decision that is clearly painful in the short term but will provide long-term benefits. Grounding your children is an example from our personal lives. You will have to make similar choices at work, especially as you're coaching someone through difficult projects and mistakes.

Try to weigh the positives and negatives benefits of each decision. Positive changes tend to compound over time, while short-term self-interest is usually in the moment. The next few minutes will be great, but then I will regret it for weeks. Doing this exercise for other people is much easier when it's not yourself debating whether to eat the slice of cake.

There's also something to be said about dealing with emotionally charged situations. Imagine that one of your team members is constantly arriving late to your weekly Monday meeting. They have done this every week for the past four weeks without explaining why. You decide to talk to them and confront them. You have two choices: you could blame them for being late or try to understand why they are late.

In the first scenario, you're likely to run into defensive walls. No one likes to be blamed or attacked. In the second scenario, you're merely trying to find the cause. You may discover that this person has been driving their children to school, and they just can't beat the traffic at this time. You may also realize that they simply slept in late every single time. Depending on the cause, you can now help them take appropriate action. Diagnose what is going on before trying to appeal to someone's self-interest.

Future

The last pillar is similar to Fundamentals, but you're looking at what might happen instead of what already took place in the future. We all make decisions based on what might be the best outcome for us in the future. We choose jobs that could provide career satisfaction, buy homes where we could raise a family, and go on vacations to places that seem fun. As you think about the future, make sure that you're considering how conditions might change.

For example, the future of music belongs to companies like Spotify. They came at just the right time and made streaming music work. The days of buying music are going away. Even Apple's innovative approach to letting you buy songs for $1 isn't viable anymore. They released their own music service, Apple Music. Any company going into this space would be operating from the assumption that streaming is the way of the future.

Consumers are willing to pay $10–$15 per month for unlimited listening and other features. Artists can then change how they release albums to match these expectations. Fewer people will go to stores to buy the album, but they will stream it. Artists could then use those streaming impressions to promote other and more profitable products like concerts, private meet-and-greets, and sponsorship.

When making decisions for the future, take a moment and think about the following questions:

- Do I know what the future might look like?
- How will current patterns evolve in the next 10, 20, 30 years, or over whatever timeline you're thinking about?
- How confident do I feel about this specific future scenario?
- If I'm looking back to where I am today, what would I do differently?

GETTING YOUR TEAM TO MAKE THEIR OWN DECISIONS

A few years ago, I was working with a client on a data-related project. We were building dashboards and helping everyone get comfortable with data. In passing, my client mentioned how he hoped that all of this data would make it easier for his team to make decisions. He was tired of having to micromanage all the decisions. This was clearly an emotional issue for him, and it took me by surprise. The dashboards ended up helping, but that conversation planted a seed for what eventually became this book.

In hindsight, the topic of this book and specifically this chapter are obvious. Making decisions is a muscle that needs to be deliberately built. I had seen friends struggle to decide where to eat or what to do in key situations. They had all the information, but it was the decision itself where they felt stuck. It was only natural that executives would struggle to delegate decisions to their teams. When I told clients about this book, they all asked me about this specific topic.

I want to share a few ideas that can help you start changing your team's rudder. If you're working in an environment where people aren't used to making their own decisions or checking every decision with their boss, the changes will take time. Just like a big container ship, you can't just turn right on a whim, but you can start the change, of course. Not every idea below will apply to your team, but there are bound to be a few relevant or that will inspire similar ideas.

Idea #1: Establish a Culture That Accepts Mistakes

Making mistakes isn't usually fatal—outside of specific fields like medicine. Mistakes can become fatal if there isn't a proper understanding of what happened and if the mistake isn't caught early enough. Look at your company's culture and determine how comfortable your team is talking about mistakes. In highly mistake-avoidance cultures, people won't make any decision to avoid the blame that might follow. They instead let someone else (an executive or the boss) make the final decisions.

To lead a culture change, you need to embody the ideas. It's not enough to just tell people to feel ok making mistakes. Set up meetings where your team can discuss candidly what worked and what went wrong. Give out an award for the most innovative idea that didn't work. Give public praise for the right effort despite the outcome. Show trust by letting others run with their ideas even if you don't think that is the right approach. Cultures reflect their leaders, and you can be the catalyst for change.

Idea #2: Teach or Coach Others How to Decide

Coaching or teaching can be highly effective for decision-making. Whether you're teaching my 3 Os framework or another framework, give people tools for understanding how they make decisions. Good coaching is trying to bring out the best in a person, and that same applies to decision-making. This is also why it's helpful to be able to explain your own decision-making process. People will want to emulate you, but it will be harder if your decision-making process is a black box.

Idea #3: Set Up Operating Constraints Wide Enough for Action

In business, there's quite a bit of talk around empowering individuals. One of the best examples of a company doing this right is Marriot. They famously allowed their employees to make any decision under $500. If a guest had an issue and it could be resolved for less than 500 bucks, the employee could do it—no need for a manager's approval or deciding on the chain. In your work, you can establish similar operating constraints. Your team could make their own decisions within specific parts of your work, specific customers, or something else.

The key here is to make the constraints wide enough to be actionable. If Marriot told employees that they had up to $50 to solve issues, they wouldn't get very far. At most, they might be able to give free meals or drinks, which many hotels do. Operating constraints can also be expanded over time as trust is built. You can work out the kinks and issues with smaller constraints and less risk.

Idea #4: Offer Data as Support

Data can help people decide. I know this from the 80+ projects that I have done exclusively on helping companies get more insights out of their data. I have worked with teams who simply needed to be presented with the right data in the right format for them to make progress in their work. I didn't have to be an expert in particular fields like paid advertising, website optimization, sales, etc. I could work with teams to organize their data, apply universal principles, and they would then take it and run with it. I could say much about the positives and negatives of data, but I will stick to its connection to data in this book. If you're interested in learning more, check out my first book, *The Data Mirage: Why Companies Fail to Actually Use Their Data.*

Within your company, aim to make data widely and easily accessible. You want people to be able to quickly generate their own reports and dashboards. You also want to make sure that people are comfortable working with numbers. Finally, make sure the data is accurate and clean. If people don't trust the numbers, they won't use them. Data can be a fantastic resource for people who aren't sure what to do and need something to provide hints.

Idea #5: Give Yourself Margins

One common pushback against letting others make their own decisions is that it will take too long. Executives tell me all the time that they don't have the time to wait until one of their team members figures this out. I'm not talking about someone who doesn't have the skills to make a decision. You can't expect a junior marketing person to make decisions at the level of a director. I am talking about someone who can make decisions but isn't able to because of a perceived lack of time.

Like you can provide wide operating constraints for your team, you can also give yourself wide margins. If you know that you would like to launch a campaign or product by a certain date, give yourself (and your team) a buffer to allow for some errors in decisions. I worked with a client who was always rushing to the next thing. He, as the CEO, made all the decisions because no one else could do it at speed he was moving. He got things done but at the expense of his teams' growth.

BEHIND THE DECISION: MLK AND THE AD-LIB

On August 28, 1963, Dr. King took the podium to deliver one of his most famous speeches. The "I Have a Dream" speech would be known globally to represent civil rights and equality. What most people don't know is that Dr. King ad-libbed the most famous lines from the speech.* The story and decision behind what is perhaps one of the most famous ad-libbed lines are fascinating.

Dr. King wasn't an improviser public speaker at this point in his life. As a pastor, he would meticulously craft his weekly sermons. He would spend 10–20 hours making sure every word made sense, and there was no fluff. He would then memorize it and deliver it in his signature style. He wasn't a man who would leave success to chance, and his public speaking style reflected that.

---

* "How MLK Ad-Libbed the 'I Have a Dream' Speech," The Wrap, accessed May 1, 2021, https://www.thewrap.com/mlk-martin-luther-king-i-have-a-dream-speech-ad-libbed/

Dr. King was forced to abandon his style when Rosa Parks was arrested and made national news. He was asked to give a speech with only a few minutes of notice. He couldn't rewrite every word and practice to perfection. Instead, he had to outline a basic speech and do his best. In this speech, Dr. King wasn't his usual charismatic speaker. He stumbled, hesitated, and the crowd wasn't working with him. However, the crowd eventually started to respond to what he was saying. He was able to notice this reaction and improvise to ride it. Effectively, he was responding to the feedback of the crowd in real time.

When Dr. King was asked to speak at the March on Washington for Jobs and Freedom, he knew he couldn't improvise this speech. He once again spent a significant time preparing his speech. The speech was well-received, but it didn't become historic until one of his friends, Mahalia Jackson, shouted: "Tell them about the dream, Martin!" Dr. King heard the comment and responded by improvising the most famous lines. Dr. King told the crowd about his dream that his four children would one day live in a nation that doesn't judge them by the color of their skin. These lines capture the audience and our imaginations for years to come.

Dr. King didn't prefer to improvise. He was more comfortable with his style of speaking preparation. Not only that, his style worked quite well! It wasn't until he was forced to improvise that he realized that he could do it quite well. He decided—albeit by force—that improvising can be the ideal approach in some scenarios. His decision to respond to the comment about the dream ended up converting this speech into a pivotal moment in history.

THE PILLARS AND YOUR PERSONAL LIFE

In your personal life, these pillars will also resonate through key decisions. Personal decisions are sometimes put off because of a lack of urgency. The lawn could grow for weeks or months; what's the worse that could happen? However, remember that decisions still weigh on us, regardless of their connection to work or not. Here's how to think about each of the pillars from a personal lens.

Speed matters in your personal life as well. I'm always surprised when I see certain personal decisions that could be accomplished in a few days, take months or years. You'll hear people talk about things they "should be doing." Momentum breeds further movement, and making decisions rapidly will give you a sense of control in your life.

Permanence is perhaps one of the most prominent pillars in our personal lives. Decisions to get married, have children, or deal with family members can have significant repercussions. Think through the level of permanence (high, medium, or low) as you tackle personal decisions.

Ownership is important to differentiate between what is under our control and what isn't. It's also easy to get caught in the problems of others, assuming that we could help solve them. Take responsibility for the right decisions and learn to selectively ignore all the others.

Loops in personal life are all of those decisions that we have to make constantly. Going to the gym, choosing what to wear, where to go on vacation, and so on happen all the time. Being able to automate many of the decisions will prove to be a big win for you. It's not just about the mental burden but about making progress on your most important personal goals.

Fundamentals aren't as relevant in your personal life, and the changes you might see—in yourself or others—will be slower. You might not notice changes every day or week, but you will see them every few years. Be comfortable adapting to the times and reinventing your identity to suit your current world.

Self-interest was made for personal life. There's a cultural perception of selfishness around doing things for yourself, but you can't help others unless you're stable yourself. Becoming more open to rewarding yourself and doing what you want can be a subtle but important change.

The future is all we think about in our personal lives. When we are young, we wish time would go faster so we could be out of school or of legal age. As we get older, we wish time would go slower to avoid the unavoidable wrinkles or adult responsibilities. Be optimistic about the future, and remember that we tend to overestimate what we can accomplish in a week and underestimate what we could accomplish in a year.

CHAPTER SUMMARY

- The seven pillars of effective decision-making are speed, permanence, ownership, loops, fundamentals, self-interest, and the future.

- Speed refers to how quickly you can make decisions. Speed is as important as the quality of the decision.
- Permanence refers to what kind of consequences might come up if we make the wrong decision. Few decisions have a high permanence, and it's important to tell them apart.
- Ownership refers to what decisions we should be making and what decisions we should let others make.
- Loops refer to decisions that happen regularly and could provide opportunities for learning for others.
- Fundamentals refer to the underlying conditions in which we are making decisions. Being aware of the fundamentals can help you avoid making the wrong decisions.
- Self-interest refers to the driving force behind making decisions that we enjoy. There's a balance between short- and long-term self-interest.
- The future refers to how conditions might change and what we should be trying to do to deal with these conditions.
- There are five ideas that you could explore to get your team to make more decisions on their own:
  - Establish a culture that accepts mistakes
  - Teach or coach others how to decide
  - Set up operating constraints wide enough for action
  - Offer data as support
  - Give yourself margins

9

Understanding Why You Made the Wrong or Right Decision

The impact of our decisions isn't always clear right away. It may take months or years before we see the true impact of certain choices. Being able to gauge the success of our decisions is crucial to improving our ability to make decisions. Without feedback, we will continue to make the same errors in judgment until they become painfully obvious.

The divorce rate for first-time marriages is well known to hover around 50%. What may be surprising is that second and third marriages have even higher divorce rates. Therapists and counselors attribute this to people continuing to marry the same "person." The things that may lead you to divorce someone may also be the things that attracted you in the first place. Without the awareness, you would continue to run this loop. We need techniques to start deconstructing our decisions.

The impact of bad decisions left unanalyzed is the clearest in fringe religions like Scientology. Scientology started in the 1950s at a time when the world was lost. We had just witnessed the deadliest war in history (WWII), and we saw the creation of atomic bombs. It might be hard to imagine today, but seeing a bomb kill hundreds of thousands of people in seconds was a life-altering event. As Oppenheimer quoted from The Bhagavad-Gita after the first test of a nuclear bomb: "I am the angel of the dead now."

The 1950s American system of health was stretched to its limits. Millions of people needed help, and there weren't enough resources to support them all. Psychotherapy was new and exciting, but there weren't enough trained therapists yet. Even today, therapy is out of reach for a vast amount of

DOI: 10.4324/9781003185383-9

people. People did trust one institution above all: churches. Ron Hubbard, a science fiction writer, came up with a method to deal with mental health challenges called dianetics. The best-selling book became a national craze akin to *The Secret* in recent times.

The book eventually fizzled out, but Scientology remained. Over time, the theory of the church became more complex, but it was still based on the fundamental premise of helping people lead happier lives. Early individuals decided to "invest" in the church. I mean this literally. Everything the church offered had a price tag attached to it. "People don't 'believe' in Scientology; they buy into it," says Janet Reitman in *Inside Scientology*.

Scientology realized that they could create a business model similar to McDonald's. The real estate in which Scientology centers are built is precious. Despite the dwindling numbers and continual bad press, Scientology is likely to be around for a long time. It has a lot of money and a small dedicated base of followers. Many people have been in it for years, but just as many have left or have been kicked out of the church. For the people who are expelled, the costs of their original decisions start to weigh on them.

Many realized that they had lost their entire social network. Scientology encourages members to only spend time with each other. Outsiders members are labeled as "Suppressive" or SP. Being kicked out from the church means that none of your friends and family want to associate with you. They also realized that their language had been hijacked. Words like "ethics" and "happiness" mean different things than non-Scientology members believe.

There is also a financial cost that becomes crystal clear after leaving. A couple who spent 34 years in the church and who made significant donations over that time were eventually expelled from the church. They realized that they had spent well over $1 million during that time. Both of them faced financial difficulties, lost their businesses, and had to rebuild their financial life. The initial decision to join a group might only become clear after other factors are dealt with.

I can't promise that this book can help people escape cults. There is an emotional context in these situations that overpowers all logic and frameworks. However, I do think that we need to analyze our decisions— good and bad—to determine where we keep making the same mistakes and what strengths we should be building on. A "bad" decision isn't just limited to the decision itself. It depends on what we do after the decision and what we learn from it. That means that every decision gives us three opportunities to maximize its impact.

There's a common adage of "learning from your mistakes" and emphasizing how they build experience. You know that, and I know that. I'm interested in how we can do this systematically and how to reduce mistakes over time. The next few pages will talk about different techniques that we can use to peek into our mental processes to remove the curtain that can sometimes blind us to the "truth" or right decisions.

DECONSTRUCTING YOUR BEST DECISIONS

Knowing why you should deconstruct your decisions and how to do so aren't the same. Everyone understands they need feedback to improve. Being able to get this feedback isn't always easy. I have seen countless examples in which people can't learn from their decisions. Most are too complex and too formal. I want to give you a few options that will cater to different preferences in learning styles. Choose the one that makes sense for you and that you will be sustainable.

Sustainability is overlooked when thinking of new ideas. Whether you're thinking about starting a new fitness regimen or starting a new marketing initiative, the excitement at the beginning will waiver over time. Think about all the conferences that you have attended where you watched a presentation that gave you amazing ideas for your work. How many of them were you able to internalize and implement? How many of them fell apart after a few days or weeks? Being able to sustain something over the long term is a better indicator of success. Most ideas will work with enough time if we give them to them.

Let's now talk about what it means to deconstruct a decision. Tim Ferriss talked about the art of deconstruction in his *4-Hour Chef* book. He referred to the "minimal learning units, the lego blocks" that every skill can be broken down into. Once you have these building blocks, you can then look at each one in isolation. Every executive that I work with is typically good at some of the elements of decision-making. They might be quite strong when choosing the right outcomes or dealing with obstacles, but they may struggle to think through all the options.

Ambiguity is harder to improve. Take a word that is quite famous right now to corporate offices: empowerment. All leaders are thinking about how to "empower" their team. The issue is that everyone has their own definition of what empowerment looks like. For some, it means never having any supervision on their work, while for others, it means being supported and guided along the way. Some managers try to empower individuals through less micromanaging.

Whenever I talk about this topic with executives, I ask them to collectively define what empowerment means. Every team or person will usually come out with a list of attributes that encompasses this word. A typical list might look as follows:

- Ability to make their own decisions
- Ability to sort through information and weigh the different variables
- Ability to recover from mistakes and choose the appropriate remedies
- Comfort voicing their opinion
- Ability to deal with others constructively and work through conflict

Once you have a list like the one above, it is much easier to work through each attribute independently. I can help any team understand how they currently make decisions and how that could be improved in the future. I could give them frameworks, exercises, and ideas that they can take into their work instantly. The same applies to any of the items listed above. By improving on these items, the overall "empowerment" will also increase. This is the power of good deconstruction and the principle that we will use with our decisions.

To deconstruct decisions, we will use a framework we learned earlier in the book: the 3 Os. As a reminder, this framework includes Outcomes, Options, and Obstacles. Outcomes are the goals that you would like to achieve. Options are the different ways of getting there, and Obstacles are the things that might get in the way of you getting there. There are several questions under each element, but the framework is simple enough to be used in minutes or more complex situations.

Using the 3 Os framework, we can take our past decisions and organize them logically. Let's imagine that you're looking to understand why a recent hire worked out so well for your team. You would use the framework to show the different variables that you considered in making this hiring decision. Your notebook, whiteboard, or mental map might look as follows.

Outcomes

- Hire a VP of marketing that can design a strategy to help us achieve a leadership position in a new market

Options

- Ask for referrals from colleagues.
- Use an outsourced talent agency.
- Put job postings on the website and promote through social media.

Obstacles

- Too many unqualified applications
- Costs of hiring role become too high
- It takes too long to find the right person

Doing this after the fact will introduce some bias. Ideally, you would note what your answers looked like before you embark on the decision. However, I'm aware of reality. You may not have done it beforehand, or you may have forgotten to write it down. You can do your best in hindsight, and you can still spot patterns in what worked well.

As with anything, we are looking for patterns and root causes. You may have realized that one of your biggest challenges in the past was getting too many unqualified candidates. It was a waste of time to interview them just to discover that they were missing critical skills. To combat this, you were going to lean more heavily into referrals and a talent agency. The first option didn't work that well, but the talent agency brought the final candidate.

The lessons would show that you were open to different options and you ran the correct math. Perhaps you avoided talent agencies in the past because of assumptions around cost or because you thought they weren't needed. You got a chance to validate these preconceived notions and see if they held up in the real world. You also have to turn frustration into practical next steps. Instead of dreading an avalanche of unqualified candidates, you had actions for how you would deal with them and alternatives for what to do if you weren't receiving enough candidates.

The process of decision-making is really a process of turning our fears and frustrations into clear next steps and backup plans. It's about managing our emotions and realizing that there are always options. We can always find ways to deal with obstacles, and it's much easier to do that before you're in the middle of the storm. A few minutes of planning can help you find alternate routes around the traffic congestion.

Let's also look at root causes in the deconstruction process. Let's imagine that you're exhausted today, and you can't mentally focus. You tried to solve that by drinking more coffee, but it didn't work. Your first thought on root causes might be a lack of sleep. You just didn't get enough shut-eye. But why didn't you get enough sleep? Well, you did watch too many episodes of your favorite TV show. You just couldn't turn it off.

The solution to tiredness is usually solved the night before or even the week before. You may need to rearrange your nighttime routine to get more sleep. Perhaps you'll need to cut out certain vices. You could also improve your diet, so you aren't as tired or need less sleep. Find the root cause of where issues went wrong and solve that problem. You're looking for the real issue, not what is easy to solve. Drinking more coffee is easy but not the true solution.

Another way to deconstruct is to get outside feedback. I was in a conference panel recently, and one of the main topics was the role of coaches. Some of my panel members were amazed at the value of a coach—despite the "high" costs. Coaching is incredibly valuable. LeBron James has multiple coaches around him, and he's the best NBA player in the world. Do you think LeBron needs help with this shooting technique? Probably not, but he's always looking for ways to improve.

A coach can be really helpful for deconstruction decisions. We sometimes get in our own way and are unable to see the truth of what happened. We may have inadvertently caused an issue or contributed to one. An outside perspective can help us take off our blinders. Freud once said that therapy was the process of turning ambiguous anxiety into crystalized fears—fears you can deal with, just like in our empowerment example.

In my work, I constantly see clients who move onto the next idea or project too quickly. They don't fully digest the lessons that should be learned. Think about all those times you spent on vacation, and you had eureka moments. I think that the mind is finally processing events and experiences. The processing is sped up when we relax. That doesn't mean that we need to go on vacation if we want to absorb lessons, but we should find time to let the body relax. It may be as simple as a walk in the park or your favorite hiking trail.

Regardless of your approach, take an active role in deconstructing your decisions—good and bad. Look for patterns and root causes to understand what really happened. Lean on others to help you see what you may be missing. Find time to let the mind decompress and process the events from your life. All of these ways will make it easier to connect the dots, as Steve Jobs famously said. The best thing is that once you connect the dots, your future decisions will be even better.

BEHIND THE DECISION: STARBUCKS FREE CONSUMER LOANS

My favorite drink is a decaf mocha with almond milk and no whipped cream. I say that shyly as I always thought it was weird that people went into Starbucks and ordered drinks that require a full minute to explain. Lucky for me, I can easily order via the app and make as many customizations as I want. I avoid the cashier interaction and simply pick up my drink. Better yet, my drink choices are saved in the app, so I can easily go back to them.

I'm sure many of us have used the Starbucks app. Perhaps even religiously. The story and purpose of this app are fascinating, though. The decision that was made to introduce this initiative turned out to be monumental for Starbucks. The COVID-19 pandemic has made the app even more important as they shift into a "convenience-led" model. Having millions of users on their app meant that Starbucks could move into a digital-first world overnight.

Let's unpack how Starbucks got here. In 2009, Starbucks started testing a mobile app for the popular Starbucks card. People used the card to store value or give them out as gift cards. It was a popular way of paying for coffee but not as convenient. What if you lost the card? How much would really load into something disposable? In 2009, mobile phones were starting to become ubiquitous, and the conversion of the card into an app seemed logical.

The app was released in January 2011, and by December of the same year, mobile transactions exceeded 26 million. The app was clearly a big hit with consumers. The app continued to evolve into what we see today. It also became a way for Starbucks to communicate promotions as seen with special "double star" days. You could even watch original video content such as the "Upstanders," which "aimed to inspire Americans with stories of compassion, citizenship, and civility."*

---

* "Upstanders Season 1 - Starbucks Stories," Starbucks Inc., accessed Aug 11, 2021, https://stories.starbucks.com/productions/upstanders-season-1/

People started loading more money into the app. You were less likely to lose your phone, and even if you did, you could simply log in to your account on a new phone. The money deposited wasn't lost, and you were never going to stop drinking Starbucks. If you wanted to pay with a Smartphone—which has become more popular in recent years—you needed the app. You can't just pay with an existing credit card; you need a balance of funds. Everyone who uses the app is depositing money.

That created a curious, positive business outcome for Starbucks[*]. They get access to money before it is ever spent. Some people might reload weekly, but others might reload every few months. I know that I have gone months without reloading, and my balance of $20–$30 just sat there. I don't mind, as I am sure I will use it in the future. Starbucks, in effect, got access to loans from their customers. The rates were fantastic—$0 interest—and consistent. In fact, as of March 29, 2020, these customer prepaid balances totaled just over $1.4 billion or 4% of the company's total liabilities.

Better yet, for Starbucks, a significant portion of these funds are not being used. If you can imagine all the gifts you ever received and how much money you "left" on the table. Even if it's only a few dollars, it can add over millions of users. Starbucks has a term for how much of these funds will go unredeemed. They call it "breakage." In FY 2009, Starbucks generated $141 million in revenue from breakage. Not bad for something consumers love. And they aren't slowing down. Since 2014, prepaid funds have grown at 10% annually, in lockstep with the company's revenue.

The decision to offer gift cards was common when Starbucks made it. The decision to jump into a mobile also made sense, though Starbucks was early in the mobile game. Ten years later, they got an amazing business unit as a side effect. $141 million in revenue is small compared to overall revenue, but I'm sure it helps with the maintenance of the app. Better yet, they are rewarded for higher consumer loyalty and revenue. It's not just a net-negative service they are offering. It also proved an important asset in navigating the COVID-19 pandemic.

---

[*] "Starbucks Devised a Brilliant Plan to Borrow Money from Customers (without Getting Anybody Angry)," Inc., accessed May 15, 2021, https://www.inc.com/justin-bariso/starbucks-devised-a-b rilliant-plan-to-borrow-money-from-customers-without-getting-anybody-angry.html

As the world went into lockdown, people still needed coffee. Thanks to the long-term adoption of the mobile app, Starbucks could instantly move into a pickup model. Users could order on the app and then pick up their coffee from their nearest location. This was already happening before the pandemic; it simply grew exponentially during it. In June 2020, Starbucks announced that it would close 400 of its US locations and look into opening stores designed exclusively for drive-through (or walk-through) and curbside pickup. They will even add dedicated pickup counters. Over 300 stores will be opened to focus on this trend.

The mobile app will be the glue that allows Starbucks to move into this new model. They will likely need less staff to run these stores while being able to deliver more orders. It also will match the long-term expectations of consumers for cleanliness. Think of how many other coffee shops will struggle to adapt to changing behaviors, and then you realize that whoever decided to launch the app in 2009 should be given a plaque in headquarters.

WHERE POST-MORTEMS GO WRONG AND HOW TO BREATHE LIFE INTO THEM (DO POST SUCCESSES)

There's something special about running a post-mortem. I think it's our innate human desire to problem-solve. If something doesn't go wrong and is important to us, we want to analyze what happened. The airline industry in the United States used post-mortems to achieve the incredible track record that we have seen in the last 15 years—no fatal crash since 2009.* Flying is generally a safe activity, but US airlines are even safer than the average. They did this by analyzing what went wrong in every accident and openly sharing the information between competitors.

We also do a post-mortem on people. When someone dies of unusual circumstances, we want to run a post-mortem. What led to the death of this person? Was it foul play? Can we learn something? There are certain

---

* "The Last Fatal US Airline Crash Was a Decade Ago. Here's Why Our Skies Are Safer," CNBC, accessed May 20, 2021, https://www.cnbc.com/2019/02/13/colgan-air-crash-10-years-ago-reshaped-us-aviation-safety.html

situations where post-mortems make sense. Most executives and leaders know and are likely running post-mortems on their biggest mistakes or failures. They want to understand what went wrong and how they could fix it in the future. The ideas in the deconstruction section are helpful here.

However, I want to make a case for why organizations should spend more time analyzing success. Instead of understanding why someone died, you would want to understand why someone has lived to 100 years old in relatively good health. Instead of looking for why a product launched failed, you want to figure out why another product flourished. What were the patterns of success? What were the reasons that led to expectations being met?

You can't build on weaknesses. That was the motto that I kept hearing from a mentor. At the time, I was in my mid-twenties, and I still felt that I could do anything if I put my mind to it. Skills were just a matter of hard work and consistency. I felt like a motivational speaker but just for myself. "Fear is just in your mind!" And yet, the idea that you can't build on weaknesses stuck with me. I also realized that there were some things I just wasn't good at. Plus, I didn't enjoy them, so the process of improving was like pulling teeth. As a side note, I had teeth pulled with minimal anesthesia as a kid, so I'm intimately aware of the pain.

The reality is that to maximize our impact on the world, we need to minimize the things we focus on. No matter how many hours I spend, I will never play in the NBA. I'm not tall enough—I'm only 5'10"—and I have barely played basketball in my life. I could be part of the NBA in another capacity but not as a player. Spending time in this area would be a waste of my time and my talents. I should seek out the things that I'm good at and build upon those. You should do the same, but post-mortems don't always align with this idea.

There are several reasons for building on strengths.

1. More enjoyable
2. Faster feedback loop as you spend more time
3. Higher impact for you and the world
4. Creates a unique advantage over others
5. Faster progress toward your goals

Great companies also follow this principle. Starbucks is building on the strength of its mobile app and moving toward a "convenience-led" mode.

Users can order and pick up orders through the mobile app. Spotify is diving into podcasts as another form of audio. Amazon is going to grocery delivery by leveraging its existing strengths in supply chains. The best companies understand their sweet spot in terms of skills and attack new markets with them.

On occasion, companies have to develop new skills to innovate. However, this adaptation takes a significant amount of resources. Think of Netflix transitioning from licensing content to creating their own in-house. Or Apple creating their own chip (M1) to replace the Intel-based ones. Or Disney going into online streaming instead of releasing content to partners. We know these companies have been successful in these transitions, but they all took years. They were a massive effort to hire the right people and shift the culture to accept these new skills.

That being said, what do we call it when we focus on success? I call it Momentum Building or MB for short. When you run a Momentum Building analysis, you're trying to understand why you succeeded and how you can exploit the reason for your success. We'll use the 3 Os framework to analyze decisions. If you do this consistently, you will start to build on your momentum. A bird can build on its momentum while flying. It can glide instead of flapping its wing. It can also dive to gain speed or slow down. Its momentum is malleable. Here are four questions to explore when running MBs.

How did you arrive at the correct assumptions?

We always want to understand how we go to specific assumptions. Was it based on experience? Did we look into the right data? Did we make the proper projections? The process of double-checking assumptions is the first step in an MB.

What surprised you?

Every success always has a few surprises. Try to identify them and determine if they were good or bad surprises. You might have encountered consumer demand where you didn't expect it. Or perhaps one of your team members did a great job on the design aspect. Surprises are great because they give you gifts that can change how you think and approach problems.

How did you adjust to unexpected obstacles?

Like surprises, unexpected obstacles are bound to occur. Besides determining why they came up, it's more important to know how you handled them. Obstacles are unavoidable, but if we feel confident in our ability to deal with them, they aren't threatening.

Based on what you now know, what else is possible?

Now that you learned something new, what else is possible? You might have discovered that your customers aren't as price-sensitive as you thought. You could now launch premium brands that will have a higher profit margin. You may also realize that your team is quite data proficient. You could seek out other insights in your data.

BEHIND THE DECISION: TRANSLATING
THE BIBLE TO GERMAN

There are few moments in history that we could point and say, "this is where history happened." The Diet of Worms is one of those moments in 1521. Martin Luther had already caused controversy by criticizing the Catholic Church and its practice of indulgences. He further hurt his cause when he made it clear that he feared God's judgment more than the powerful men in front of him.

There are many things that Luther did that led to our world today. Luther set the foundation for our idea of oneself and created a world where multiple religions could coexist. He almost single-handedly created the "voice of the people" and the way it could impact governments and organizations. He changed how Christians thought of their religion and would eventually influence other religions.

Of all his actions, the one that stands out the most to me is his translation of the Bible.[*] At the time, the Bible didn't actually play an important role in the life of an average Christian. Most bibles were written in Latin, and most people didn't know Latin. Bibles were seen as books that highly trained monks or priests could only read. Luther,

---

[*] "The Bible Translation That Rocked the World," Christian History, accessed May 25, 2021, https://www.christianitytoday.com/history/issues/issue-34/bible-translation-that-rocked-world.html

being one of those monks, read the bible intensely. His reading of it is what led him to challenge the Catholic Church and the status quo.

He told Christians that all they needed to know was in the Bible. These were the words of God, and you shouldn't have an intermediate like the Pope tell you what's in it. The trouble is that bibles weren't accessible. Besides the language barrier, book printing wasn't scalable. The launch of the Gutenberg printing press coincided with pivotal moments in Luther's life. In fact, he used printing to share his ideas throughout the entire European continent.

Naturally, Luther wanted all Christians to know what he knew. He wanted them to be able to read the words of God themselves. So he decided to translate the Bible in German and specifically into the kind of German spoken at the time. The project was incredibly ambitious and took him a few years to complete both the New and the Old Testament. Once the Bible was in German, the knowledge was set free, never to be contained again.

Luther wasn't the first to translate the bible into German. There were at least two earlier translations, but his fame and language choices made it the most adopted. His translation was so influential that it directly influenced the evolution of the German language and other versions such as the King James Bible. He severed the relationship that many Christians had with the Vatican and created the Protestant movement that still lives today.

It may be hard for us to grasp the impact of this single action. By this point in history, Christianity was the dominant religion. Luther split it into many variations and flavors. Christianity would continue to spread even further now that every single person could actually read the bible. Eventually, other versions in English and other languages would be created. Our world would never be the same.

Today we are typically unaware of the influence that Christianity has over our world. It is so all-consuming that we might not see it. Think about how we measure time. When we say that this year is 2021, we are saying that we live 2,021 years after Jesus Christ was born. The label of "The West" is simply an area west of where Christ was crucified. We swear on bibles before testifying in court. Even our ideas about human rights and equality come from the seeds of Christianity. It's unclear if the religion would have kept spreading at the same rate without accessible materials and books.

Next time you pick up or see a bible, remember that this was possible because of Luther. His obsession over what was the right way of worshipping God changed his world and ours. His translation of the bible may be the most enduring and visible consequence of his ideas and decisions. Those small decisions have snowballed into our life, whether we see them or not.

THE FALLACY OF DECISION JOURNALS AND REDUCING ANALYSIS FRICTION

For years, the Roman Emperor Marcus Aurelius woke up and wrote into his journal. He captured ideas that he wanted to remember and wrote down reminders. For example, he would write something like this to remind himself of how to act.

"The things you think about determine the quality of your mind. Your soul takes on the color of your thoughts."

I don't think he ever expected these thoughts to be public. To him, he was just writing in a private diary how to be a better person. Yet, his writings are one of the most popular books available today. They have become an essential read in Stoicism philosophy, and we now get to peek into his inner thoughts. It's not every day that you get to read the literal thoughts of the most powerful person in an empire.

Journaling has been around for thousands of years, ever since paper became affordable and widely available. Depending on your perspective, you might think that keeping a diary is an essential way of processing life's events or something that you only do as a child. The value of journaling should be obvious to you now. Being able to capture our thoughts on paper makes it easier to understand them. It's harder to organize them in our heads, especially if there is a high emotional connection.

I don't personally keep a regular journal, but I do use one from time to time. It's beneficial whenever I feel rushed, frustrated, or stressed. I'll notice some tightness in my chest or jaw, and that's my cue to pull out my journal. Over a few minutes, I can write down all the things that are bothering me. One by one, I can see if there's evidence to support this feeling, or if I'm imagining things. I'll occasionally use it to deconstruct decisions and what worked well.

In the world of decision-making, journals have become popular. They are called "Decision Journals," and you can find many templates online. You could print them or simply copy the structure—usually questions—into a new notebook. The promise of decision journals is that they will help you become better at making decisions. I see where they are coming from, but I think these journals have a few fatal flaws to address in this chapter.

The first fatal flaw comes down to consistency. The most valuable thing about deconstructing decisions is that you can do it often enough. The format and questions aren't as important. I talked about using the 3 Os as a simple format, but if you tweaked this to something else, that would still be fine. The main problem we want to solve is reducing the friction it takes to analyze decisions. If we don't, then only the most successful or most embarrassing decisions will be analyzed. Think about people who only start thinking about their romantic relationships after going through a painful divorce.

If we let emotional weight determine what decisions to analyze, we will continue to make the same mistakes for months or years. Decision journals have too many questions, in my opinion. It can feel like you have to complete homework or an evaluation every time you want to analyze a decision. If you're the type of person who enjoys the structure, then decision journals are perfect for you. Find the best format and start using it.

For everyone else, think about how to reduce the friction in your analysis. You might put a note in your office with the three questions or points to think about. You might have a reminder in your calendar to go through these questions. Or you might develop a shorthand for capturing written ideas. Whatever works for you, it's fine. The goal is consistency, not perfection in the analysis. If you can tie it to an enjoyable outdoor walk, even better.

The second fatal flaw of decision journals comes down to the structure. I mentioned that I think they have too many questions. The problem with this is that we dilute the learnings. If you have ever attended a conference or workshop, you know what it feels like to be overloaded with new ideas. One good idea is better than ten okay ideas. Being able to internalize that one idea can be more impactful than trying to level up across multiple areas.

B.J. Fogg, a social scientist at Stanford, talks about "tiny habits" in his online course and books. He discovered that for habits to stick, you should start with tiny actions. Instead of flossing your entire mouth, start by flossing one tooth. That may seem pointless, but you're trying to develop the habit, not achieve perfection. If you can consistently floss one tooth, and then two and then three, then you can eventually do the whole mouth daily.

The process of habit learning is relevant for us here. I always recommend to clients to start with small changes that can take place often. There's value in being able to lock yourself in a remote house in a forest over a weekend to analyze your decision habits. Suppose you can do this every weekend, then more power to you. However, you can also make tiny analyses on a daily or weekly basis. You can then pick up seemingly small lessons that can compound into major changes.

For structure, you can start with the 3 Os. If you feel comfortable with more questions, then add them. If not, you can even look at just one of the Os (Outcomes, Options, and Obstacles). To make things even easier, you could use the structure of what worked, what didn't, what did I learn. Memorable and simple is better than complex and comprehensive.

The third fatal flaw of decision journals is the requirement of the written word. Being able to write our thoughts is actually a relatively new occurrence. For hundreds of years, people spoke about their ideas. Think about Aristotle, Plato, or any Roman senator. Before paper was widely available, speaking was the way we communicated and worked through ideas. I meet many people who aren't comfortable writing even bullet points. That's fine. You can take advantage of a highly honed human skill: talking.

Without writing, decision journals may not be as useful. Instead, you could complete entries using your voice. Simply record yourself answering questions. Most phones support the ability to transcribe a voice memo, or you could easily find services online. You can then store these voice memos in a digital notebook or your computer. The point, once again, is to make it easy. Speaking through the 3 Os framework can feel like a breeze.

The fourth fatal flaw of decision journals is that they create a crutch. I think frameworks and guidelines should be like training wheels. They help you learn the basics of how a bicycle works, but you eventually want the freedom to ride without them. Writing down or speaking through thoughts is helpful, but you also want to learn how to do this mentally. That is the ultimate way of reducing friction. Some decisions may be too complex for a mental approach. You can always fall back to writing or speaking. Nonetheless, mental deconstruction is the final skill we want to learn.

If you're the type of person that can benefit from decision journals, then you likely skipped this section. For everyone else, remember that the goal is consistency. We achieve that by using a memorable structure and finding the right medium—writing or speaking. Over time, we are building our mental ability to deconstruct decisions in our minds. The learnings will compound over time, and you will be glad that you started with tiny actions.

CHAPTER SUMMARY

- Deconstructing our best and worst decisions exposes us to ideas that we should fully internalize.
- If you only do this once in a while, your rate of learning will be lower.
- Ambiguity is hard to improve, but if you break that down into specific skills, you now have good starting points, e.g., deconstructing empowerment.
- Use the 3 Os as your structure for deconstructing decisions.
- Post-mortems are fine, but spend more time on Momentum Builders (MBs). Build on success, not failure.
- Decision journals can work, but the goal is consistent analysis. Make it simple and memorable.

10

Trusting Your Gut in a World Ruled by Data

When I entered the world of data six years ago, I would have never expected some of the learning that I would eventually encounter. I'm constantly asked by prospects and clients why I became an expert in data. The story takes some unusual turns, but it will provide the necessary context for this chapter.

When I was 15, I was fascinated by the internet, specifically, the business portions. The idea that you could create your own online store, sell products, and then get paid seemed like magic to me. I had to learn how to code to take advantage of this amazing opportunity, so that's what I did. There were a few resources online, and I started teaching myself what today we would call frontend development skills.

I remember coming across a CMS (content management system) that seemed perfect for one of my projects. The issue is that the CMS was only available in German, so all the documentation had to be translated (before Google Translate existed). On an average night, you would find me staring at my computer, trying to build websites, reading a German website, and trying to translate it into English. I would eventually come across other CMS like Joomla and WordPress, which were just getting started.

I naturally started doing freelance work once I picked up a few skills. I loved the freedom of choosing your own projects and having to tackle different challenges each time. Eventually, I discovered that I didn't enjoy staring at code all day long. It was fun every once in a while, but I was more interested in the marketing side of things. I wanted to make a switch, but I didn't want to "lose" all that I had learned as a teenager. That's when I discovered the world of analytics.

DOI: 10.4324/9781003185383-10

Data seemed like a highly technical field but mostly used by non-technical teams like marketing and sales. I understood the technical details quickly and thought that I could help companies by helping them translate their data into something useful. In my first book, I talked about becoming a Data Marriage Counselor, mediating between teams like engineering and marketing. I could talk to both sides and helped arrive at the same location.

Over time, all my client work shifted to analytics, and I stopped building websites except for my own business. After working with data for years, I concluded that the technical details were actually the easiest. Making choices on technology, implementation, and debugging were straightforward things. Dealing with the human element of data was a whole different story. I constantly came across teams that were overwhelmed with data, had trust issues, or were simply afraid of numbers.

You couldn't throw technology at a psychological problem, and that's what some vendors were doing. They promised heaven and earth without telling companies that they would have to deal with cultural issues before being data-driven. My work was basically validating their choices of technology and then helping them sort through how to get people to actually use all the data they were collecting. All of this naturally led to decision-making. Once you have data, you're likely going to use it to make better decisions. No one wants data as a goal. It's always a means to some end.

In this chapter, I want to share my latest thoughts on the role of data in decision-making. It has been almost a year and a half since I wrote my first book, *The Data Mirage*, and I have continued to refine my approach to data. As you can tell by the chapter title, I don't think we should rely exclusively on data. I think numbers can live in harmony with intangibles like a gut feeling. In fact, I think data can help train your intuition, something that the best executives are doing and most people completely miss.

I love the world of data. It still captures the magic that I felt when I started building websites when I was 15. However, I don't think it is a silver bullet or the most important thing that companies should be focusing on. It has an important role but a limited one. This chapter will show you how you can start trusting your gut in a world ruled by numbers. You will learn to use data while still sticking to all the ideas covered in previous chapters.

IN GOD WE TRUST, ALL OTHERS BRING DATA

Sometime in the last 100 years, Edwards Deming uttered a quote that will be used constantly when talking about data: "In God we trust. All others must bring data." Companies and executives use it to justify why their companies should keep investing in data. People use it to argue against opinions without any evidence.

I think Edwards Deming had the right intention when he said this, but the essence has been lost in today's world. Data is important, but it is not the most important thing that your company should be focusing on. Data is a lever that can make other things easier, not the end goal in itself. I have talked about creating data-supported cultures for years now, and that's quite different from data-driven cultures. In the first one, data supports decisions whenever possible, while data is the only way of making decisions in the second one.

Our data-driven world has swung too far in one end of the pendulum, and we need to correct it. Let me share the seven most persistent myths that I constantly encounter when I talk with executives about data. We need to rearrange our compasses before we can start talking about the more practical uses of data.

Myth #1: Data Is the Most Important Resource

The Economist dedicated an entire issue to talk about how data is the new oil. They were, of course, talking about companies like Google and Facebook—who have turned data into multi-billion dollar empires. For most companies, these aren't role models. Almost everyone else is really into creating great products/services and delivering those to happy customers. Data can help, but it is not your product.

For Google and Facebook, data is their product. They want to capture as much as possible and then sell it through advertising. For other companies, data is merely meant to help you support your decisions. Strive to build data-supported cultures, not data-driven ones. Give yourself room to make decisions without data; it won't be the end of the world. The COVID-19 pandemic forced companies to make decisions without data.

There weren't enough numbers that could explain what the drop in demand might mean for countless industries. The car industry, for example, expected demand for new cars to drop when the pandemic started, so they reduced their production capabilities. They turned out to be wrong and soon found themselves dealing with a global crisis in critical parts. They had the wrong decision-making process, not a lack of data.

Myth #2: Collecting Data Is the Hardest Problem

After years of technology evolution, data collection is, in fact, the easiest challenge for companies. Everyone is drowning in data, and the onslaught isn't stopping. Knowing about your customers is easier than ever. This is why the conversation has shifted from "how do I collect more data?" to "how do I store it and access it rapidly?" Conferences now focus more on data warehouses, data lakes, and anything that could help companies surface more insights from their ever-increasing pile of data points.

The ease of collection has made other problems worse: we can't process data fast enough, we get easily overwhelmed, and we can't separate the truth from the noise. Some people expect technologies like AI to solve this problem, but that's unlikely to happen. You can't throw technology at a psychological problem. If we could, we would have cured anxiety disorders, depression, and other mental health problems. Companies need to get smarter on helping their people understand numbers and use them regularly.

In your company, focus on how many insights you're regularly learning. Whether those insights come from billions of data points or a handful, it doesn't matter. How is your data helping you change your behavior? That's the true benchmark you want to be used to gauge your success. If it happens to include advanced ideas like AI and machine learning, then fine, but remember that behavior change is the consequence of good data practices.

Myth #3: Everyone Wants to Be Data-Driven

There's an idea that everyone wants to be data-driven. Just give them the ability to make their own reports and dashboards, and everything else will take care of itself. In my experience, this has not been the case, though perhaps I operate in a different world. I come across many people who aren't comfortable with basic statistics, probabilities, and numbers in general. It reminds them too much of math class back in school, and they don't want to revisit those times. Some people want to have the insights and not have to show their work to the teacher.

Your company should be planning for all these use cases. Make it easy for people to export data into CSV and other raw formats, and make it easy for people to get insights without running complex formulas. Data democratization is about reducing the barriers for people to interact with the data, but nothing says that everyone needs to become a math whiz. I have come across executives who want to be knee-deep in their data, but I also know executives who just want the insights. Both approaches are fine and should be supported by your company.

Myth #4: Machine Learning Is the Future for All Companies

There's a lot to be said about machine learning and the world of AI. For starters, the world isn't as new as we think. We have been working on AI since the 1950s, and even then, we were apparently only ten years away from self-driving cars. The world of machine learning did go through a significant shift in the last 10–15 years as cloud computing became accessible at scale. The real use cases are hiding behind all the hype that follows whenever anyone talks about AI. Generally speaking, anything to do with pattern recognition, fraud, and analysis is a good challenge for machine learning.

Focus on how these use cases will help you achieve strategic goals. Why go through all the effort of creating models if they aren't going to help with revenue, market position, reputation, or something tangible? Save your research energy for problems worth tackling. There are countless innovation opportunities within your company regarding how you deal with customers, ongoing changing consumer behavior, and overall industry trends. Be an expert at finding and jumping on them.

Myth #5: Technology Is the Trickiest Part of Any Data Strategy

Most of the prospects who reach out to me come because of specific technical questions. Should we use vendor X? What if vendor Y doesn't work for us? I understand their frustrations. There are hundreds of options in any given category, and they are all quite similar. Making the wrong choice seems like a huge waste of time and resources.

However, don't confuse volume with priority. Sorting through vendors can be tricky, but it's also the last step in any data strategy. Start by figuring out your people's role with data and how you will convert data into insights (process). Then, you can see what role technology can play in helping you with the first two items. Going through this process actually makes technology selection easier because it narrows down space. The choices left will match your company's unique makeup and approach.

Myth #6: Facts Are Clear, and Everyone Can See That

"Show them the facts" seems to be the rallying point during the COVID-19 pandemic. Look at the case numbers, and you will see everything you need to know. As it turns out, everyone interprets facts differently, and the same happens within companies. I have been in board meetings where facts were presented, and executives extracted different lessons than I thought. Any fact will go through a psychological filter based on our experience, biases, and desires. Your data strategy should take into account how the human components change how facts are perceived. Don't assume that everything is black and white.

Myth #7: Opinions without Facts Aren't Welcome Here

I respectfully disagree with Edwards Deming. I don't think you can discount opinions that don't have as much evidence behind them. If an executive with 30 years of industry experience suggests an idea, are you going to dismiss it because of poor evidence? Isn't his/her experience the data? There's a pushback against things like intuition and gut feeling, but I think they play a role in how we make decisions. Ensure that your company can allow opinions, or you will lose a big chunk of experience and "hidden data."

Data is playing a huge role in how companies innovate. Continue to invest it, but do it delicately. Don't get caught up in the hype and try to put the wrong expectations on the data. Remember that data is just one part of how we make decisions, and it's not the end-all for most companies. Perhaps it is time for us to increase our trust in ourselves and our opinions.

DEALING WITH THE DATA TRIFECTA

I was recently giving a presentation to a small group of executives from mid-size companies. We were talking about data, and I had prepared a few ideas that I thought would be helpful to them. A few minutes into the presentation, I realized that many of my points weren't that interesting. Instead, they wanted to talk about what you can do once you have too much data. They were drowning in numbers and wanted someone to toss them swimming jackets.

This presentation took place early in my data practice. At that point, I was focused on helping companies track more data and improve their technology. I hadn't realized that this wasn't an issue for most companies, especially companies doing well. These companies had already invested significant resources into their data infrastructure. They were tracking millions or billions of data points in real time and with some of the best technologies. Their challenge was actually using the data to make better decisions. They had this amazingly fast, modern car that no one knew how to drive. Just like you might admire a nice car once you walk by it, they were simply admiring their data infrastructure.

Over time, I learned that three major problems prevent companies from using data to their full extent: overwhelm, lack of trust, and silos. I call them the Data Trifecta, and I can almost guarantee to find at least one of them when I talk with a prospect. You'll realize that these three challenges are psychological in nature and can't be easily solved by technology. In fact, technology might make some of them worse by increasing the volume of data that comes your way. You can't drink water from a broken fire hydrant, and that same applies to data (Figure 10.1).

The Data Trifecta is rooted in human psychology. In my first book, I briefly covered biases that get in the way of using data. Some of them are likely familiar to you. Confirmation bias, sunken cost, and confounding are a few of the examples. The fundamental challenge with data is that while technology consistently gets better every year, our human minds aren't adapting quickly. Companies can easily collect billions of data points, but we will struggle to work with more than seven data points in our short-term memory—think of trying to remember phone numbers.

Executives are then presented with a huge amount of information with no instructions on sorting through it. Some companies are leaning on

Data Trifecta

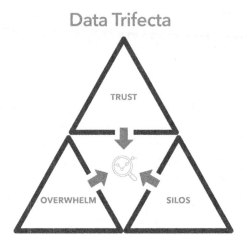

FIGURE 10.1
Data Trifecta.

tools like machine learning and AI to sort through their ever-increasing pile of data, and that will be helpful in specific scenarios. However, it is important to understand how you can help your team easily swim through data to find those actionable insights you were promised during the many vendor meetings you participated in.

Data Overwhelm

The first challenge of the Data Trifecta is overwhelm. This is the classic "walking down the cereal aisle" problem. Imagine going to the supermarket to buy a new cereal. You don't know what you want and instead will decide once you get there. The only problem is that there are literally a hundred choices of cereal at your local store. They all look surprisingly similar, and they might even cost roughly the same. How do you make a choice when everything looks the same to you?

That's the problem with data overwhelm. You're confronted with so many data points that you're not quite sure what is important and what is noise. You may have discovered that 40% of your customers went to law school but so what? Should you change your marketing campaigns to talk about the law, or should you just ignore this insight? Now multiply this by ten, 50, or 100, and you start to see the difficulties. Who's to say what is important or who could provide the authority?

There are four strategies that you can employ to deal with data overwhelm: gatekeepers, WDIM, three things, and expectations. The underlying principle is to reduce the overall volume. It's not about designing a process that could accommodate the weighing of hundreds of variables. It's about reducing the number of variables that you're working with. You want ways to rapidly remove large swaths of possibilities, so you can deal with the remaining few.

I usually get pushed back at this idea. Executives expect some kind of magical formula that can be applied to all of their data and spit out the right answer. They basically want a magic eight ball that considers all variables and then just tells them what to do. Instead, I want them to work with fewer inputs to produce more outputs which are decisions in this case. Once they get moving in a direction, it is much easier to redirect the momentum toward the correct destination.

The first strategy to deal with overwhelm is to employ gatekeepers. Companies are trying as much as possible to reduce friction in accessing data, but in some cases, you want to add friction. Some companies make it too easy to create reports, and everyone is constantly looking for them without thinking through what they actually want from them. If you're interested in learning more about the location of your customers, what will you do with the information? If you don't have a good answer, your fishing expedition might prove fruitless.

Going fishing isn't bad, but if your team struggles to sort through all the noise, you need to become more deliberate in where and how you fish. Gatekeepers can simply ask a few questions to clarify the overall goal of creating a report. You want your own devil's advocate who is skeptical of data requests. The Catholic Church created this position to argue against any given individual's canonization (sainthood). They would assign someone to literally "advocate for the devil" (or against God). The healthy skepticism ensured that facts were uncovered and observed.

The second strategy is to obsess over WDIM, which stands for What Does It Mean. Whenever you come across an insight like the ones I mentioned in this chapter, your team should start debating what this insight means (WDIM). If you can't come up with good answers, you may be dealing with a vanity metric. Vanity metrics are interesting to look at but don't actually mean much to your business. If a metric can go up or down without forcing a significant behavior shift within your company, then you can safely ignore it.

The third strategy is "3 Things" and is the simplest. If you can't seem to figure out how to prioritize your data, simply pick the three things that fit the best or seem the best to you. You can then analyze these three things further and take action on them or discard them. Wrong choices are seldom fatal, but paralysis is. Getting moving can be incredibly helpful because you can now gauge the impact of your decisions and adjust as needed. Picking three things and moving is sometimes the easiest.

The fourth strategy is managing expectations. For some teams, having the pressure of delivering on a deadline is the thing that helps them break through overwhelm. They focus on prioritizing, making clear choices, and finding the WDIM in their data. Work with your teams to manage expectations around how data is used and the different scenarios in which data is appropriate, and where it can be safely ignored. If you expect data to be used everywhere, you will eventually run into issues where a lack of data is holding you back.

Funky Data

The second challenge of the Data Trifecta is lack of trust or Funky Data as I call it. I started to notice this issue when clients would tell me that the reports or dashboards in front of them didn't look quite right. There was something funky about them. It first drove me crazy since I was personally involved in the calculation of these numbers. I always had to go back and double-check all the formulas before I could tell them that the numbers were, in fact, correct.

Over time, I realized there were three reasons why clients ran into Funky Data: technical issues, misaligned expectations, and unexpected calculations. Technical issues are what everyone tends to default toward. There's something technically wrong with the data, and the "bug" needs to be fixed. In some companies, specific teams or people might be blamed— typically engineering. While technical issues might be the root cause, it's not the most common one in my experience. Technology is getting better every year, and these kinds of bugs are disappearing.

Technical issues are also the easiest to solve. It's just a matter of tracking down the bug and squashing it. The bug may be complex if you're dealing with advanced infrastructure, but the solution is out there. You need someone capable of sorting through all the connections to determine what could be causing the missing data and then provide a fix. When I come across bugs, I'm relieved because I know that the steps to solve them are going through a technical process.

The second reason behind Funky Data is misaligned expectations. Companies or teams that haven't used much data are highly susceptible to this issue. I have come across teams and executives who tell me that their customer conversion rate is "around" 10% or that their customer churn is "roughly" 5%. Someone did some math (unclear how) to come up with this number, and it has become a rule. When someone like me comes in and looks at the latest data, the real number might be completely different. It may be significantly higher or lower, and that wasn't the expectation.

The longer that this expectation has been set, the harder it is to change it. As you can imagine, the solution here is primarily psychological. You need to present new evidence that backs up why the "new" number is real. You may do that by showing the limitations of the previous analysis or showing a thorough analysis of the current data and the factors that contribute to the number in front of them. Over time, expectations can be shifted, but it may require a constant prodding or explanation of the new numbers.

The third and final reason behind Funky Data is unexpected calculations. In my experience, this is the most common issue that teams run into. Any KPI, report, or dashboard in front of you is just a series of calculations. Some of them are quite simple, but most will have FYIs that you should be aware of. For example, even a simple number like # of online purchases could be different from what you expect. The KPI might exclude mobile purchases because those are considered different or exclude repeat customers (only look at new customers). Don't assume that everyone in your team or company is using the same language. I have been in rooms where everyone talked about customer retention differently, for example.

Data Silos

If you have ever driven by a modern farm, you have likely seen huge metal cylinders—twice as big as a house—shining on the horizon. These huge structures are called silos and are used to store grain and other materials. In companies, you can also find silos, but they aren't as obvious or even remotely useful. Data silos in companies represent different sources of information that aren't able to mix. Marketing will have some data while sales will have other data. Their data complement each other and provide a different puzzle piece, but you would never know because no one has bothered to combine the data for unified analysis.

Silos are the third challenge of the Data Trifecta. They have existed ever since teams were created. Some people believe that silos were a technical problem. It's too difficult to combine the data from different departments. There's no easy way to unify multiple data sources. We know now that this isn't true. Technology, as I have said multiple times, is rarely the issue. It might be the case if you're trying to build level five self-driving cars, but those are the exceptions that prove the rule. Silos are fundamentally political and people problems. It's a lack of desire that keeps silos separate, not a lack of technology.

For my clients, I have often played the role of a "Data Marriage Counselor." It fulfills a fantasy of mine to be a therapist sitting across someone talking through their life problems. I haven't quite done that, but I have done something similar with different teams within companies. Like in therapy, I work with both teams to figure out the problems and how they can compromise to a solution that benefits everyone. Teams don't help each other for a multitude of reasons. They don't have the time, it's not in their self-interest, there are political considerations to keep in mind, and general jockeying for power. My goal is to cut through all of this noise and get teams aligned on sharing data. I might not get the teams to like each other, but I can get them to work with one another.

In your company, consider establishing a similar role. This person wouldn't represent any team and would move throughout the organization with minimal friction. Their role is to help each team be more impactful by giving them better data. Some teams might have more data to give, but everyone can benefit by getting access to other data. I worked with a company where the sales team wasn't privy to marketing data. They just saw prospects appear out of thin air within their CRM. By simply getting them to know what campaigns drove specific prospects, they could change their conversation approach. Marketing benefited by tweaking their campaigns based on what the sales reps were seeing on their end.

The second way to break through silos is by adopting a culture of WDIM. Every data point or question should go through the What Does It Mean question. Why do we even care about this point? Tech startups have come up with what they call the "North Star Metric," which is the one metric that really matters in the early stages. North Star metrics are too simplistic in larger organizations, but the intention is not. Unify teams along with metrics that make sense for both of them. Customer support and operations can talk about happy customers. Sales and marketing can talk about qualified leads. Engineering and product can talk about customer experience. By focusing on the WDIM, you can help teams see how their work is similar instead of separate.

TRAINING YOUR GUT WITH DATA

Beethoven is one of the most well-known artists in all of history. His name has become synonymous with classical music, and we have all heard one of his songs though perhaps we didn't know it. What may surprise you is that Beethoven started going deaf when he was 30 years old. By the time he was 45, he was almost deaf, and yet, he wrote some of his most famous pieces after losing his hearing, including the Ninth symphony. Beethoven used to put a pencil in his mouth to feel the resonance of the piano to compose songs.

It was clear that years of training had ingrained Beethoven's ability to compose music. It was such a deeply acquired skill that he didn't even need to actually listen to the music to know if what he was creating was great. His intuition had been finely tuned for years, and he was now able to reap those rewards to avoid a career-ending situation such as losing his hearing. It's important to note that Beethoven was able to keep creating music but wasn't able to play at concerts, a significant portion of his income. Nonetheless, the role of intuition is fascinating to watch in his life (Figure 10.2).

We can think of the role of data and intuition using a classic 2 × 2 chart. In the far right corner, you have high data and high intuition which makes you data-driven. Both elements are being used in harmony. On the bottom right corner, you have high intuition and low data and you would be gut-driven, e.g., whatever feels right. On the far left corner, you have high data and low intuition which would make you numbers driven, e.g., accountants. On the bottom left corner, you are low data and low intuition, and you're simply emotion driven.

You would likely switch between quadrants in different areas of your life, but you're aiming to be in the top right for the critical decisions. Too

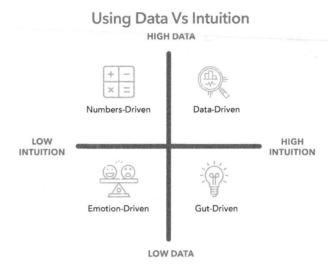

Using Data Vs Intuition

FIGURE 10.2
Data vs intuition.

much data and you can lose track of the qualitative element of decisions. Too little data and you can lose track of the entire picture. The harmony of decisions starts by balancing both of these elements.

Intuition or gut feeling annoys scientists because it isn't easy to measure. It may even be seen as "woo-woo" and something that has no concrete meaning. We can understand hard skills such as math and science, and we have even converted softer skills like music and sports into concrete blocks that could be analyzed. Intuition might be under attack, but I don't think we should dismiss it altogether. My background in data leads people to assume that I do not believe in gut feeling and that everything has to be backed up by numbers. I don't know how anyone could spend any amount of time working with data and come to such a conclusion. There's only so much we can learn from data, and there are instances where we have to rely on our intuition.

I take this one step further. I think data is a fantastic tool for training our intuition. In your toughest situations, all you will have is your gut feeling. Basketball players have to determine how to take the last shot of the game. Executives have to react on the spot to questions from investors and other shareholders. Children will ask for your opinion and advice at any time. You can't tell people to hold off for one minute while running a data analysis to determine the next step. Everything in this book is about honing your decision-making ability so you can use it spontaneously and across any situation.

You can start to see a similar approach take place in sports right now. For years, athletes were coached by humans on how to improve their mechanical skills. Baseball pitchers would get advice on how to improve their pitching, basketball players would deconstruct their three-point shot, and golf players would tweak their swings. We are now seeing an increase in wearable devices that can do all of these skills and more. I talked to an expert in baseball pitching coaching, and he was sharing how pitchers are now using special balls that capture all kinds of data and share it back with the pitcher. Pitchers could now practice on their own and use the data to tweak their approach.

I love this hybrid approach because it uses data in a way that is useful and immediately applicable. The baseball pitcher can look at the data and convert those insights into mechanical motion. Eventually, the pitcher can internalize the more efficient movement so they wouldn't need the data. We don't want the pitcher to rely on the data in a real game. Instead, we want to use practice time to learn new movements that can be translated into the real world. That's what I'm referring to when I walk about using data to train your gut feeling.

Let me now share three strategies for how you could replicate the baseball pitching example in your life. We don't all spend our time throwing curveballs, but there are plenty of opportunities to use data to hone our intuition.

Strategy #1: Validation of Assumptions

The first strategy is to validate assumptions. For example, let's imagine that you're about to start the process of launching a new product. You should make a list of all the assumptions that you currently have about this product. You may think that this product will be a hit among the 18–35 demographic and do well among California customers. You may also assume that it will take six months to fully launch it, and your biggest obstacles will be around branding. We all have these kinds of assumptions, but the key is to write them down to not forget them. It is difficult to separate our original assumptions from the real answers because we constantly reevaluate our perception of the world. By the time the product launches, you may forget all about your initial ideas.

It's also helpful to expand on why you're leaning toward a specific assumption. You may be bullish toward the 18 to 35 age demographic because you currently have two similar products which perform well there. You also think the style of the product fits into what you know about this specific age demographic. By expanding on your assumptions, you start to peek into your thought process. The actual thought about choosing this age demographic might have been nearly instantaneous, but your mind did actually process some kind of information to get there.

Keep a record of these assumptions as you proceed through the product launch. As new data comes in, you want to compare notes. If it turns out that the product did quite well among the 35–50 age group, then you want to understand why and what was the missing piece in your assumption. The real-world data may show your expected age group was willing to spend money in certain areas, but they didn't consider your product essential while the older group did. Don't feel bad if an assumption was proven wrong. Get excited because you can figure out the kink in your thought process.

In a way, this is how experience is developed. We assume an approach or idea will work, we try it, and then we learn whether we were right or wrong. Someone with 30, 40, or 50 years of experience in their field has gone through thousands of assumptions and proven them right or wrong. If we can consciously take over this process, we could learn much faster. Learning is blocked by rejection or dismissal of new evidence. If you simply conclude that the changes in age demographic were a fluke, you might make the same mistake in the future. Managing your ego is critical to allowing this process to happen rapidly.

Strategy #2: Lean on Others

Another strategy to train your gut involves leaning on other people, specifically people with different personalities or inclinations. If you're someone who has a bias toward data and evidence, find someone biased toward their intuition. The same would be true of the opposite. I constantly come across executives who have a bias but haven't done anything to explore other ways of making decisions or building their assumptions. We usually hear about exploring other points of view, but I think it's just as important to explore other decision-making styles.

When leaning on others, focus on a similar question or, ideally, the same question. You can see how other people approach it and how they come up with their own assumptions. Depending on your style, you will have to do some prodding into how someone arrived at a specific conclusion. Remember that the thinking process can happen quite quickly, but there are a series of data points considered to arrive at any assumption.

A great real-life example of this strategy can be seen in Bridgewater Associates, the hedge fund founded by Ray Dalio. Bridgewater is one of the largest hedge funds in the world, with $150 billion in assets under management. It also ran under unique management principles covered in a fantastic book: *Principles* by Ray Dalio. One of the many principles encourages employees to dissect each other's thinking to understand how they arrived at specific assumptions.

Employees can then capture these conversations in an internal app called "Dots." These conversations are then used in other reviews to discuss what happened and how their decision-making can be improved. The culture at Bridgewater is brutally honest and open, and people self-select themselves to be part of this massive experiment. I don't think all companies can adopt this kind of mass transparency and push back, but you can control what happens within your team and handle feedback.

One of the things that I helped executives do is to expand their style of decision-making. I'm not trying to correct weaknesses, but I think we can improve our how-to approach decisions by understanding how others would act in our situation. The less abstract this is, the better. The most effective approach is to have someone in your team or company go through assumptions and ideas in real time as they happen. This makes it easier to validate our approach and see where we can make improvements.

Strategy #3: Play Devil's Advocate

The final strategy to consider is playing devil's advocate to others ideas. I spoke about the origin of this phrase originating from the Catholic church and how they would assign someone to argue against the canonization of a specific individual. You can adopt a similar approach in your team meetings. Too often, everyone jumps behind an idea simply because of group pressure or because the idea came from their boss. Executives are always telling me that it's hard for them to find people who aren't simply going to say "Yes" to everything that comes out of their mouths.

The kind of pushback needed to make this strategy work needs some seeding on your part. In your meetings, you can assign someone to play the role of a devil's advocate. In this role, the person would be responsible for finding why something won't work within reasonable parameters. It's not about shooting everything down but trying to find the holes that may be overlooked in all the excitement. Make sure that someone captures the objections and those that should be addressed regardless of the outcome.

The key to making this work is to start small and provide your blessing. Bringing this idea to every single meeting that you're involved in will cause your entire team or company to grind to a halt. However, you can start by adopting this idea in your strategic meetings, especially when you're deciding on a new approach. It's at these points when you need a devil's advocate the most. Having someone pushback on minor tactics isn't going to be as helpful, especially once you're trying to gain speed.

The second aspect is providing your blessing. We all act based on the actions that are happening around us. You may have values on a wall, including one that reads "We openly challenge each other," but if someone does this and they get reprimanded, you can be sure that they won't follow the words on the wall. Make it clear that this is something you want and that won't cause any issues. If possible, go first and play the role of devil's advocate.

If you haven't come across as open to feedback in the past, you will need to work harder to get this adopted. Your team might have learned to avoid giving you feedback because of how you might react or what you might say. Communicate that you're working on changing how you receive feedback and that you will be asking for it going forward. Do your best to manage your reaction, especially if you're hearing things that you weren't expecting. Like any skill, it gets easier as you practice it.

BEHIND THE DECISION: LOOKING FOR THE ROOT CAUSE OF DEATH

"Every year that you're alive, your risk of dying increases by 10%." That's the starting line to a fantastic article from the Wall Street Journal titled "The Best Remedy for Our Diseases? Aging Less."* In the article, the author argues why we should focus on figuring out

---

* "The Best Remedy for Our Diseases? Aging Less," *Wall Street Journal*, accessed May 25, 2021, https://www.wsj.com/articles/the-best-remedy-for-our-diseases-aging-less-11618003335

why we age instead of merely tackling the symptoms of aging: cancer, heart diseases, etc.

As it turns out, not every animal ages in the same way as humans. Some turtles, fishes, and mole-rates all aged very slowly. Their cells don't deteriorate with the same consistency that human cells do. A 100-year-old turtle would be quite similar to a 20-year-old turtle in terms of the age of their cells. Their mortality rate is driven by other factors like predators and the environment. We aren't quite sure why they don't age like us but the answers may be critical for our lives.

The challenge with old age is that it usually comes with multiple diseases, all of which can kill us. An average 80-year-old is suffering from at least five different diagnoses. Even if you could successfully cure one of them—such as cancer—you would still have four other ones to contend with. We saw this in the COVID-19 pandemic as people with multiple comorbidities were more susceptible to the virus. A weakened immune system is a perfect target for other diseases.

There are calculations that even if we could completely cure cancer, we would only add around three years to the average life expectancy because of this multiple diagnoses challenge. This doesn't even consider the damage that could be leftover from cancer treatments and the kind of quality of life that people could expect. The root cause is to slow down aging, so diseases like cancer never take hold. Humans might still live a similar length, around 90 years, but the quality of those years would be higher.

In the United States, aging causes 85% of all deaths but only receives around 6% of all the government health research funding. Aging hasn't been considered a viable topic to explore, and we have focused primarily on specific diseases like cancer and Alzheimer's, which can be caused by aging. There is a balance of what is practical and doable, but as we saw in the COVID-19 pandemic, humanity is capable of amazing things if you're able to focus resources and time.

The conversation around aging reminds me of what we discussed around problem-solving. It doesn't matter how hard we work at something if the work itself isn't focused on the right problem. How we make decisions isn't just for work but for everything we do. Perhaps our next century will be more aligned on slowing down aging as a way of tackling all the diseases that keep killing us.

LIVING IN HARMONY WITH NUMBERS

I was recently engrossed in a conversation (close to an argument) with someone about COVID-19 vaccines. Specifically, we were talking about the AstraZeneca vaccine, which has been linked to blood clots. To the other person, the blood clots were extremely worrying and showed that these vaccines were rushed. I thought these side effects were expected, and they weren't significant. "It's basic statistics," I was told. Was it truly basic statistics?

It made me think of how we deal with probabilities and how we manage risk. There's an assumption that we logically process risk and then make the best choice. In reality, I think that we are irrational when it comes to risk and will actively choose riskier activities for many factors. Why do we do this? Control.

No commercial airline in the United States has had a fatal crash since 2009, and in fact, over the past 12 years, US airlines have carried more than eight billion passengers without a fatal crash. Before you bring up the Boeing 737 MAX recent accidents, it's important to know that these took place outside the United States with primarily non-US citizens. Even including those still means that flying is one of the safest activities we engage with regularly.

The amazing safety record came from three simple ideas: extract lessons from crashes, share them among all companies, and work with them to make voluntary changes. Mandatory regulations can work but aren't as effective as voluntary changes. All airlines wanted to be safer, and it was in their best interest to make these changes. And yet, we fear flying. Have you ever found yourself in turbulence? Had a rocky landing or take-off? I would bet that you had a moment of fear as I have experienced it.

I think we fear activities like flying because we don't control them. We are merely going along for the ride. If a plane was to crash, we could do nothing but hold on tightly to our armrest. We will gladly choose control over risk. Driving feels exponentially safer to us, but the statistics don't back that up.

The AstraZeneca vaccine seems to cause blood clots five times in a million. How high is this number, and how does it compare to other things we do? According to car insurance companies, an average driver will crash once every 18 years. Everyone will experience at least three collisions per year and perhaps more depending on your driving skills and those around you. The chances of dying from a car crash are 1 in 103.

One in 103 vs 5 in 1,000,000. The difference is that car crashes are under our control. "Who knows what went into a vaccine?" That's the general thought process. Statistics are rarely simple.

Life isn't risk-free. We are reminded of this every time a seemingly "healthy" friend gets cancer or suffers a heart attack. We always wondered how that could be if the person did all the "right things" like eating well and exercising. Sometimes you're at the wrong place, wrong time. You're walking along a street that you have walked hundreds of times, and you get hit by a car or get fatally robbed.

The question isn't how we avoid risk but how we manage it. What's the evidence that we have, and what is riskier. The AstraZeneca vaccine has risks, but suffering from COVID-19 might have higher risks in the short and long term. Don't fear risk. Accept it and move on.

Numbers might be one of the most useful and enduring inventions that humanity has ever come up with. Ever since the Hindu-Arabic system swept over Europe, our lives have been surrounded by numbers. You can't go more than a few minutes without seeing numbers. Time, directions, business, finance, and others rely on numbers heavily. We take for granted the role that numbers play in our lives, and we haven't properly developed the right tools for dealing with them.

In your personal life and teams, strive to learn fundamental skills to avoid falling prey to the biases I mentioned at the beginning of this chapter. You can't simply choose to "avoid" numbers or have someone else deal with them. We all need a few skills that can allow us to fully interact with our world and make better decisions—the whole point of this book. Just like a musician has to learn to first learn the rules before breaking them, we must first understand how numbers work before deciding when to ignore them. When executives ask me about skills their teams should work on, I give them the following list.

1. **Statistics**: when Donald Trump won the US presidential election, most models only gave him a 5–10% chance. Some even gave it less than 1%, but those were running more on biases than science. Nonetheless, Hillary Clinton seemed like an assumed win. Her loss shocked many people, especially before we learned about the limitations of polling in this election. There was also a lack of understanding of basic

statistics. A 10% probability is low, but it will still come up once in every ten chances. It's not impossible but somewhat unlikely.

2. **Expected Value**: building on the first point, probabilities and expected value are helpful skills to know. If something is only 20% probable but has an expected value of $1,000, it would be reasonable to spend up to $200 trying to get that outcome. On the other hand, if something has a probability of 10% and an expected value of $100, you should only spend up to $10 working toward that outcome. Probabilities are common in business, but the expected value isn't always clear. Without knowing that, you could be spending into an abyss without the possibility of making a positive ROI.

3. **Comparisons**: data on its own doesn't mean much. China reported fantastic economic growth in the first quarter of 2021, but their numbers rely on comparison to the previous year in which growth slowed down to historically low levels. Any kind of improvement would have been seen as amazing. The same is happening with inflation as I write this. We had a period of deflation at the start of the pandemic, so prices rising now have an "inflation" like quality. Only the long-term data will show if inflation is a concern.

4. **Patterns**: you need three occurrences before a pattern starts forming. Someone late to a meeting doesn't have a "pattern of being late" until it has happened three times or more. Be good at noticing when patterns are forming and when people are assuming that there's a pattern if the data doesn't support it. Patterns can show long-term opportunities, but they can also show our bias to connect the dots regardless of how they fit together.

5. **Biases**: psychological biases affect all of us, and they have been covered to death in other books. Be aware of the most important ones and how they are manifesting in your team. Some of the ones you will encounter include our tendency to confirm our beliefs, our desire to find patterns, our belief in our opinions, our perception that adding is better than subtracting, and our weaknesses to overvalue recent evidence.

6. **Visualization**: most of the data you will see will appear in charts. Understand how charts come together and the different ways in which scales, design choices, and the underlying data can communicate different meanings. I have also noticed a tendency to

treat charts with a sense of importance because someone went into creating them or because we assume that visual data is more truthful than raw numbers.

To live in harmony with numbers, we also need to put data into a broader critical thinking process. I was recently conversing with someone who didn't quite believe that our province, British Columbia, was testing upwards of 10,000 people every day. This person thought that if this was true, we would be seeing huge lines of people lined up waiting for the test. We both knew people who had been tested, so we had anecdotal evidence that there weren't huge lines taking place at the testing center. It was more likely to wait in line at Costco than it was to get a COVID-19 test. The "basic math" didn't add up.

The question stayed with me, so I looked up the data to understand how the number could be true. It's important to give enough energy to both sides: why could this number not be true, and why could it be true. In this specific example, I started by confirming the number of people who were being tested every day. It hovered around 10K for weeks and months, so it seemed like the data was stable. I then learned that the province had set up around 110 testing centers. Some were existing medical clinics, and others were brand new COVID-19 centers. This meant that every center was processing around 90 tests per day on average.

Each center has average business hours of 9am to 5pm, which means that every center processes around 11 tests per hour. Each test took around five minutes, which means that if you walked into any given COVID-19 testing center, it was extremely likely that you would be the only person there or, at worst, might be waiting behind a handful of people. Huge lines of people would be an anomaly and would only happen if only a few testing centers were in the entire province. To further understand the point, I then looked up how many Starbucks exist in the province. As it turns out, there are also around 105 stores. Starbucks likely serves 10,000 people every day without forcing customers to wait in long lines.

If we want to use such a grandiose word, the research took five to ten minutes. I then took the data and ran it through some basic critical thinking to determine what is likely and what isn't. Based on the numbers, 10,000 tests per day isn't strange, and in fact, the number could likely be even higher without ever seeing the anecdotal evidence of "long lines." Think of how much time is wasted worrying about "fake" testing numbers when you could determine the validating in just a few minutes. The missing piece isn't data but a critical, objective way of dealing with it. Most of the decisions that we are confronted with aren't complex, but we add complexity by injecting emotion and preferences.

BEHIND THE DECISION: THE RISE OF QANON

On January 6, 2021, a crowd gathered outside the United States Capitol. The day had been talked about for months in online forums, and the crowd—soon turned mob—came together to protest the defeat of Donald Trump in the 2020 US presidential election. The plan on how this protest could actually turn back the results wasn't quite clear. Eventually, the crowd breached the security perimeter outside the Capitol and came inside the building. Senators and Congressmen had to be evacuated to safety, and it took hours before all the protestors were removed from inside the building.

The storming of the US Capitol had been prophesied for years by an online group called QAnon.* The group gained notoriety in the previous two years and, at its peak, had millions of followers. The story of how QAnon came to be is a fantastic study of how seemingly small decisions can eventually snowball into huge real-life consequences. The event on January 6 showed the ever-increasing power of our modern world and the things that we will need to keep in mind in the future.

QAnon started around 2017, but its origins can be traced back to much earlier. Online forums where members can post anonymously have been around since the internet started. One of the original forums was called 4chan and was founded by a user named moot. The forum allowed any kind of speech as long as it wasn't illegal. At any given time, you could find racist comments, pornography, and some of the vilest discussions going around in 4chan. The success of the website spanned competitors, including a site called 8chan. The principles and ethos of all of these sites were the same: free speech, anonymity, and low friction of posting and reading content.

On October 28, 2017, a user named "Q Clearance Patriot" appeared on one of the boards of 4chan. He posted a thread titled "Calm Before

---

* "QAnon: What Is It and Where Did It Come from?," BBC, accessed June 1, 2021, https://www.bbc.com/news/53498434

the Storm," where he talked about a future event where alleged suspects would be arrested, imprisoned, and executed as child-eating pedophiles. Q, as the user would become known, would continue to drop these "Q Drops." The messages were cryptic by design, and they were supposed to be analyzed and researched by regular users. Over time, a following developed for Q and his/her drops. Every message was scrutinized and deconstructed.

The cryptic nature of the messages made it easy for anyone to attach any meaning. Phrases like "10 Days of Darkness" could be applied to multiple scenarios. When something happened in the real world that matched a message from Q, all the users celebrated. When something didn't happen, it was seen as a fluke. An entire community developed around Q, including YouTubers, Twitter accounts, and other social media personalities who spread Q's messages and meanings. Eventually, Q was banned from 4chan, but the user moved toward 8chan, where the messages continued. The group, the supported Q, came to be known as QAnon.

During the COVID-19 pandemic, QAnon activity nearly tripled. With everyone in lockdown, surrounded by a global event, and full of uncertainty, it seemed like Q had been right all along. The pandemic was the calm before the storm, and the upcoming US election in November 2020 was a key event that had to be won. Keep in mind that Q had talked about special "events" taking place in previous days, which didn't happen, November 3, 2017, January 20, 2021, February 1, 2018, February 16, 2018, and so on. The list of dates that were missed was staggering. The conspiracy theory simply kept moving targets.

Everything changed after the US election. Trump lost by a thin margin in the electoral college, and he outright claimed that the election had been stolen from him. QAnon took this as a sign that they should ramp up their activities in the real world. All of this came to a tipping point on January 6, 2021. Unlike previous events, people actually showed up in person. Trump himself encouraged protestors to take back their country, which was the final push QAnon supporters needed. The plan, if we can call it that, failed. There was even another date that came and went: March 4, 2021. The movement lost steam but still has thousands of people who follow and believe in it.

All along the way, we see thousands of people make micro-decisions to support and engage with the movement. They shared a post on social media. They told a friend. They watched a video. They took evidence against the movement and dismissed it. All of these micro-decisions affected others and compounded into what we saw on January 6. Like a pinball machine, the effect of all of these micro-decisions was impossible to predict. We don't have good solutions to how we deal with misinformation and conspiracy theories, but I think we can start by understanding what is influencing our decisions and how we are handling evidence that supports or rejects our fundamental beliefs.

CHAPTER SUMMARY

- Data isn't the most important resource, it's merely another tool to help you make better decisions.
- Facts aren't clear, and they are morphed by our emotions, preferences, and biases.
- Proactively deal with the Data Trifecta: overwhelm, trust, and silos. Most of the solutions here are people-driven and not limited by technology.
- Using data to train your gut is one of the most underrated benefits that executives and people miss.
- Use three strategies to train your intuition: validate assumptions, lean on others, play devil's advocate.
- Learn to live in harmony with numbers by working on six skills: statistics, expected value and probabilities, comparisons, patterns, biases, and visualization.
- All data should live within a broader critical thinking process. That's the missing piece.

Conclusion

The Greek word for the process of decision-making is "euboulia."* It refers to the deliberation that should take place when thinking of a decision. We see it in the *Iliad* and a few writings from Plato. Like other ideas from Greek philosophers, clear instructions are provided for how to deliberate, how to verify information, how to consult others, and much more. The art of decision-making like so many other things, is as old as time.

In this book, we have covered a lot of ground. We started by shifting our world of decisions to include our personal lives. Decisions are rarely just limited to one domain, and the process of decision-making can be applied to anything once you learn it. Wins in your personal life can transfer to your work life and vice versa. It makes sense to look at your entire life and not just a subset of it.

We then worked through the three strategies for dealing with the avalanche of decisions that we face regularly: Elimination (problem-solving), Automation, and Optimization (3 Os). Each one requires a different approach, but they can be seen as sequential. Strive to work only on the right problems. If possible, automate decisions. If you can't use the first two strategies, use a framework to get to the best outcome. Large brushes at the beginning and small brushes toward the end.

We covered decisions that changed our world or our understanding of it. The entirety of history could be viewed purely through decisions. Why did someone choose to start a company? What led rulers to act against their people? These decisions aren't always simple, but they help us understand the complexity that takes place. We can see the emotions that drive them and how they dealt with (or ignored) facts. If nothing else, they are incredibly interesting to study and think about.

We then spent a couple of chapters diving deeper into how decisions get made within groups and how to be leaders. For some people, the main role of an executive at any level is to make decisions. You might have some hands-on work, but your highest impact comes from choosing the right

---

* "Euboulia in the Iliad," Cambridge University Press, accessed June 1, 2021, https://www.cambridge. org/core/journals/classical-quarterly/article/abs/euboulia-in-the-iliad/84230361B01715C0700B8 9AC8DEF017B

DOI: 10.4324/9781003185383-11

direction and what to work on. Sometimes these decisions aren't easy. Worse of all, it can feel like you're making them on your own. Learning to make decisions under pressure is an invaluable skill for any leader.

We also spent time looking at post-mortems and the different tools that can be used to analyze decisions. While helpful, I think we want to work to internalize skills. Training wheels are useful at the beginning, but you eventually want to ride your bike without them. The freedom is worth any stumbles that may happen as you get rid of them. Don't let frameworks become crutches that slow you down or prevent you from being in the moment. There's a time for training and a time for performance.

As an expert in data, I had to include a chapter on intuition. I work with many executives who are data-driven who eventually run into decisions that require something else. Data isn't everything. There's a fine balance between using data and being reliant on it. You want to walk that tightrope confidently, and the last chapter shared a few ideas on how to do that best. Our world is trending toward being more data-driven, and these balance skills will be even more useful in the future.

It's been a pleasure to write this book for you. I hope you enjoyed it as much as I did writing it. I don't expect you to internalize everything, but if you got an idea or two out of it, that's a win. If it made you think of things differently, that's also a win. Our journey to understand decision-making continues. As a species, we are getting better at it even if it doesn't seem like it. I wish you the best of luck in mastering the art of euboulia. You can bet that I will be working on the same skill.

Appendix

There are free newsletters, audio, video, and other materials available on my website: http://rubenugarte.com

You can dive deeper into how to make better decisions by exploring the resources that I built for this book at this link: http://rubenugarte.com/BulletproofDecisionsAppendix

Index

Printed in the United States
by Baker & Taylor Publisher Services